FINDIN

IN THE

LOVE

&

HIP HOP

ERA

FINDING <u>REAL LOVE</u> IN THE LOVE & HIP HOP ERA

CHRIS SAIN JR.

FINDING REAL LOVE IN THE LOVE & HIP HOP ERA

In the *Love & Hip Hop Era* a lot of people don't believe marriage is still important. I strive daily to be a positive example for others. It is important for me to show them that LOVE is real and still exists by treating my marriage like it means the world to me.

Contents

Introduction

When we love God, we'll love others, because that's the way real love works! However, it seems as if in today's world, we are looking for love in all the wrong places. I coined the term 'Love & Hip Hop Era' years ago as a way to define the era in which we live in today. The book, ***Finding Real Love in the Love & Hip Hop Era***, was birthed because I've seen in record numbers (in my workshops, classes and speaking engagements) both men and women alike, quitting on friendships, relationships and marriages. Long gone are the days when people would fight for love. Long gone are the days when people would fight for their relationships. Nowadays, at the first sign of adversity, couples are throwing in the towel, unwilling to work it out, unwilling to go through the storm, unwilling to grow together. Quitting in general has become the accepted norm for our world today.

It seems as though best friends have turned into strangers. Those that don't know you support you and congratulate you more than the people that do. It makes one wonder, what happened to love? It's like real love no longer exists. Showing love is now seen as a sign of weakness. Hate is the new love. In the *Love & Hip Hop Era*, the hate be so real and the love be so fake.

Above all else, we are expected to love each other deeply. See, real love, I am talking about genuine love, knows no boundaries. When you really love people, no sacrifice is too great. We have become a selfish people. But, love is patient. Love is kind. Love is long suffering. Real love does not envy. Real love doesn't boast. However, often times today, some people only show love when they feel like dealing with you. People don't even speak anymore. Why? Because the *Love Factor* is gone. The *Love Factor* has been lost.

Love is extensive. Love is expressive. Love is expansive. Love is not jealous when others love the ones we love — love WANTS others to truly love the ones we love.

I sat back one day after receiving over a thousand Facebook inbox messages. With over 200,000 fans on social media and a constant barrage of messages daily, I was only able to read about a hundred messages. Doing my best to reply to as many as possible, which is how I built my organic social media following, I paused for a moment before completely stopping altogether. The common theme in the messages I read and was able to respond to, was all about relationships, breaking up, love, and should I stay or should I go? I thought to myself, Lord, why me? Out of all people, why have these people found solace and the comfort to reach out to me about their relationship issues? God responded, why not you. So, after meditating on God's word, praying about what I should do (after all it is a huge responsibility to have so many people trust and confide in you), I came to the conclusion composing my would-be responses into the basis for my second book. Sometimes we have to go to that quiet place to hear from God. He whispered to my spirit, 'Go and bless my people with the words I have placed in your heart.'

Contrary to what the media and magazines say, I am not a relationship expert. I have never subscribed to that title. I am a guy that really had 'em; a guy that really lived out the experiences in which I talk and post about on social media as it relates to love and relationships.

Dating in the Love & Hip Hop Era

Tempted by all the wonders of the world, I thought deeply about whether or not a relationship was for me. I remember as a kid being so turned off by marriage because of what I had seen modeled in front of me. I can vividly remember thinking to myself growing up, as I watched my mom and dad in what seemed like a forced relationship they called *marriage* (that was void of love and compassion say) 'If this is what being married is all about, I don't want any parts of it.'

Of course I grew older, I grew wiser and began to experience love and relationships on my own terms - no longer needing to use my parents' relationship as a barometer and the end-all-be-all to relationships. I jumped off the porch and began to develop my own thoughts around relationships and what it meant and whether or not it was something I wanted to participate in.

I've always had a way with ladies. I enjoyed what many would consider one of the most legendary runs as a high schooler. I was primed and prepped to have as many women as I could…simply because I could. I knew no boundaries. Later in life, I would learn the principle that everything that is permissible is not beneficial. Only when I began to mature and strengthen my spiritual walk did things change. Life began to run its course. I began to see things a little clearer and suddenly having all the most beautiful women in the world no longer mattered. I took a step back and started to reflect.

Love & Hip Hop Era questions that I ask myself:
When did it become cool to date your best friend home girl? When did it become acceptable to sleep with someone else's baby daddy? When did it become honorable to listen to all her relationship problems and turn around and put her through the same thing now that you two are together? – Just questions that I asked myself. The sad thing about all of the questions I have is the fact that all of this is now the norm. All of these things are socially acceptable. Wrong has become the new norm. Wrong is now the accepted way of living in the *Love & Hip Hop Era.*

I have established a resume that left me conflicted. Through one set of eyes, I'd be revered as arguably one of the greatest playboys ever. Through another set of eyes, I am easily one of the biggest whoremongers of all-time. Not proud, nor ashamed. I guess it is safe to say that I was who I was and now, I am who I am. And, I am cool with both of those people. By no means does it make me an expert on love and relationships but, it certainly qualifies me to share my perspective; a perspective that may be life changing for someone.

Dating multiple women has become the accepted norm in the *Love & Hip Hop Era*. Women know about each other and many of them don't care. Expectations and value systems in both men and women have changed; self-respect is at an all-time low. What good is being a 'dime' if your self-respect isn't worth a penny? Who will value you if you don't place value on yourself? Some men have completely lost their way. We have some fathers who have abandoned their own kids to take care of children that do not have his DNA. And to be clear, I am not saying anything is wrong with taking care of kids that are not your own, but don't do it at the expense of neglecting your own kids. A man is someone who can take care of himself or any condition he creates. Anything else means you're male by gender.

Through observing millennial couples (young couples between the ages of 16 to 25) I noticed that while dating, many of them don't know how to love. Many of them don't know what love is. Many of them don't know what real commitment is or consists of. Many young couples today like the idea of love; they like the idea of a relationship, but are unwilling to put in the necessary time to make it work. Young couples today, are not willing to make the necessary sacrifices to cultivate a healthy relationship. One of the main reasons why love has eluded young couples dating in the *Love & Hip Hop Era*, is due to the examples many of them are emulating. In our communities, many times within our own families, we see on an everyday basis, toxic and unhealthy relationships. Some men have multiple women they are dating, that live across the street and around the corner from each other. Some women have a 'work boo' (this is someone who is considered your work companion/boyfriend while at work) and then go home to a live-in boyfriend who refuses to work but sits around and plays Madden, NBA 2K and Call of Duty all day. Some men won't work because some woman have allowed that man to sit at home and be a bum. It is sad and unfortunate that some women just want to be able to say to their friends and family that they have a man…knowing that that man won't work, doesn't work and refuses to work. They fully know and accept that he smokes weed all day and can at times be abusive - verbally, physically and emotionally. *Love & Hip Hop Era* women allow this…that is the sad part. Another reason why love has eluded young couples dating in *the Love & Hip Hop Era* is the influence of what they see or perceive to be the lives of reality television. Unaware of the fact that a lot of what they watch and see related to relationships are intended for ratings and views. Women disrespecting women, arguing, throwing drinks on each other, unable to communicate like mature adults have become the preferred way of communication for girls growing up today in the *Love & Hip Hop Era*.

Marriage in the Love & Hip Hop Era

I'd be the first to admit that I thought that I was the least likeliest guy to every get married? For some reason, I never thought marriage was quite for me. Ever since undergraduate school, I have thought of myself as a well-to-do individual with or without a wife. I was (and still am as I pen these words) young, educated, athletic, handsome, confident, makes an honest and successful living, stable with consistent income, own my home, own my car, great health insurance, life insurance, investments, driven and ambitious. 'Settle down for what?' was the question that I used to ask myself?

I would soon learn however, all the success in the world means nothing if your life is incomplete. All the success in the world means nothing if you have no one to share it with or to create memories with. In the *Love & Hip Hop Era* we are surrounded by pretty women. That makes it that much more difficult to settle down with just one. Although I had narrowed my choices down to about a handful of women I deemed worthy of marriage, I had one in particular that settled at the forefront. She was the one God clearly designed for me. We met while attending Michigan State University (MSU). Even back then, there was something special about her. However, trying to develop something deeper with her was put on hold as I continued my quest to entertain as many women that would entertain me. There was a Bad Boy R&B group named 112 who put out a hit song years before my time, but it rang true to my thoughts and feelings about marriage and this one special lady:

'When I do get ready to settle down, Baby, the first one I am calling is you.' – 112

Sure enough, after I completed my college football career and earning my advance degrees, I hit her up. I called to check to see if she was in a serious or committed relationship. She wasn't. I checked to see what her interest level in me was because I knew she found me attractive before. I also knew she connected with my energy, but now, some time had passed. Actually, years had passed and it was important for me to see what kind of feelings, if any, she still had for me.

We began dating and that eventually lead to us getting engaged. After being engaged for about a year, we got married. For me, it was a process, however, I knew all along she was the one I would marry. All men know. Whether or not they act on it and take that next step is a totally different thing. My delay for marriage was more about me getting myself mentally ready to spend the rest of my life with one person. I have always dated quality, strong and well-to-do women, so my options were filled with other women that I could have seen being my wife. That was one of my challenges to committing to marriage in the *Love & Hip Hop Era*, committing to one woman.

With all that being said, being young and married in the *Love & Hip Hop Era* has been great. Although it does come with its share of challenges and temptations. Living in the world we live in today with social media providing access to a plethora of beautiful women thanks to Instagram, Twitter and/or Snap Chat, marriage is something that brings calm and peace to a world that constantly wants to get lit/turned up. I believe successful marriages last if and when you love and trust your wife, have a generally healthy relationship and a genuine desire to make it work.

The *Love & Hip Hop Era* however thrives on the belief that half of all marriages end in divorce. With perceived odds that terrible, it has provided justification for couples to shun relationships and quit on marriages. Getting divorced has become the new fashion statement. Research has identified the following qualities associated with more stable marriages: good communication, conflict management, emotional support, happiness, dedication, and a willingness to sacrifice. To those not yet married, research also identifies a couple key components that can help your future union last.

1. Be careful when deciding to live with each other. Living together before getting engaged is linked to divorce because sharing a home makes it harder to break up. A joint lease can lock you into a relationship and increase the chances that you'll end up staying with—and marrying—someone who isn't right for you.

The better choice is to wait until you know he or she is the one and have a mutual interest in spending the rest of your lives together.

2. Talk about your future expectations before saying 'I do.' 'Where do you want to live?' 'How many kids do you want?' 'Who will work and provide?' 'Who will stay at home with the kids?' Having these tough and courageous conversations can reveal whether or not you are a good match for each other long term. For some people, this may lead to what I call 'smart breakups' instead of toxic marriages that end in divorce.

Part 1

Trading Respect for Attention

May I remind you of something you already know? The currency for today's individual is social and it's all about attention. Take a moment to think about what people value online. They equate value to the number of likes, shares, views, retweets, reposts, etc. All of these measurements are about someone paying attention to what they said. It feels as though getting attention is so rare today that people are crying out for it sometimes, even begging for it.'

A strong woman, who won't jeopardize her self-respect, can get any real man to love her. However, when you lower your standards and stop respecting yourself, he will run all over you and leave you for a woman that will make him respect her. Sometimes the person you want doesn't deserve you. Why? Well number one, he doesn't respect you. Please don't feel like you are respecting your man by allowing him to disrespect you. A woman has to be willing to lose her man in order to keep her man. If a man doesn't feel that a woman will ever let him go, then he will never respect her enough to stay.

Love for one another is so far gone, people are *'doin them'* at the expense of trying to fill a void left by the people that should be loving and supporting them. This emptiness is the void that many unknowingly walk around with today. Regardless of how good you look in that selfie or how nice that outfit is, no filter can fill the void left inside of you. One must connect with their true self. One must seek to find and discover their true calling and strive to fulfill their purpose on this earth.

Love is so absent in our lives that people are abandoning friendships because someone did not 'like' their Instagram or Facebook post. People are quitting relationships because they are in a real life relationship but online looking and acting like they are single. People are ending marriages because instead of investing and working to strengthen their own marriage, they are busy watching someone else live their life. More often than not, they do not know or have a clue about what other couples go through and/or have went through to arrive at where they are today. These things are the results of lack of love, lack of affirmation, lack of affection, lack of appreciation and lack of attention.

During the *Love & Hip Hop Era,* **respect** has all of a sudden became the character trait of choice to sacrifice while in search of something with a deeper meaning and a deeper purpose. The *Love & Hip Hop Era* has provided fuel to the ever burning fire by creating a culture in which respect is out and getting any type of attention is the new love. The *Love & Hip Hop Era* has produced a selfish and self-serving group of people. All they care about is living for today and living for themselves, nobody else. Live fast, die young is the motto. You only live once (Yolo) is the mantra. The reality of it all is that it is perpetuating a cycle of broken people raising broken people. The same is true for hurt individuals as well; hurt people hurt people. If a man really wants to be with you, you will know it. If you have to question it, let it go. Don't let the person that doesn't love you or respect you keep you from the person that will.

#MCM

The perfect guy is not the one who has the most money or the most handsome one you will meet. He is the one that knows how to make you smile and take care of you each and every day until the end of time.

A Real Man: Is honest. Takes care of his kids. Gives up his seat for a woman. Tells the worst truth instead of his best lie. Listens. Reads. Is well groomed. Is secure enough to have her stand in the limelight. Smiles. Is romantic. Minds his manners. Holds doors open for others. Is trustworthy. Is on time. Loves and respects his parents. Makes mistakes. Doesn't hold mistakes others make against them. Understands that he doesn't know everything. Makes a conscious effort to learn something new every day. Loves hard and says what he feels.

Too many woman are claiming men that don't belong to them as their Man Crush Monday (MCM). Too many women are in relationships with men that are single. Sadly, many women are lusting over men that don't claim them and that won't even bring them around family and friends. Ladies it is best to find you and keep you a man. What you have with your significant other is not for everybody. You and your man should both have this understanding. Unfortunately, too often time only one party gets the memo while the other is cruising through making you look like a fool.

See a real man would never hide his relationship with you. A real man that is God centered, will allow you to come to his home, introduce you as his woman, speak of you to family and friends and show you affection no matter who is around because he is proud that you are his woman. It is no secret. Men go hard for what they truly want, so ladies, if your man is not going hard for you, then you are not what he truly wants. If you keep pretending their actions doesn't hurt you, the only person you are lying to is yourself. Know your worth. Make sure your MCM feels the same way about you. More importantly, make whoever your MCM is that he belongs to you and only you.

What a shame it is that we hurt the ones who loves us for the one who don't love us at all. A good man doesn't play games with your heart. In fact, a good man will cut off any female that threatens his relationship with his woman. Unfortunately, the Love & Hip Hop Era has told society that it is okay to play with your love and manipulate your heart. In the end, we all just want someone that chooses us over everyone else, under any circumstance. Sometimes to be truthfully honest, it is better to just remain single. I believe being single is better than being lied to, cheated on and disrespected. Our actions help create insecure women. As men we complain about the things we don't like in women but in reality, we played a role in some of that. The deepest of a woman's insecurities often times come from the men who have hurt them.

#WCW

When you love you, you won't tolerate someone else mistreating you, disrespecting you or isolating you, because when you love you, the person you love has to meet your expectations. I believe Women Crush Wednesday (WCW) was birthed because love was absent. When love is absent we tend to supplement our desire for love with faulty things. I remember vividly when the hashtag #WCW became a phenomenon. It was a sad day in the *Love & Hip Hop Era*. I remember how so many pretty girls and bad bi$c%es were begging to be some man's WCW. For months, I observed women on various social media platforms, like Facebook and Instagram, wait in anticipation for Wednesdays to roll around in hopes that some random man, that they didn't even know, would make them their Woman Crush Wednesday. It got so bad that women started begging to be a random man's #WCW. Women started getting stressed. Many became bitter and hurt. Why? All because love was absent. When love is absent, women in particular began to search for love in all the wrong places. Many hurt and bitter women started making Facebook statuses late Tuesday night stating 'I hope I am somebody's woman crush tomorrow.' Sad!

When a woman is loved correctly, she becomes ten times the woman she was before. If she has a job, her own car, pays her own bills and is out here doing her thing, understand she wants your loyalty, honesty and commitment; not your money. Don't deny her the opportunity to decide what is best for her by lying about your true intentions. Sometimes, men will do anything to get what they want even if it ruins woman's heart. Daily, I pray that every woman with a good heart puts her heart in good hands.

My wife is the only women I'm crush'n on. She is my Woman Crush Every-day (WCE) all day. The Love & Hip Hop generation has, in some ways, shown no regard for the covenant of marriage. In the world today you have married men crush'n on other married women. You have married men claiming other women, often time celebrities and entertainers, as their woman. Where they do that at? Dude, you are married! You exchanged vows with your wife not those Instagram models. Many men have also lost their way. It seems as though everything is permissible in the Love & Hip Hop Era…but not everything is beneficial.

You don't have to be looking for love to appreciate the good in a person. Sometimes you just need a friend who 'understands you', someone who can be close to you without becoming a burden on you. Connection matters. Make time to have something real, be patient and let it grow. One day it just clicks. You realize what is important and what isn't. You learn to care less about what other people think of you and more about what you think of yourself. You realize how far you've come and you remember when you thought things were such a mess that they'd never recover. And then you smile.

You smile because you are truly proud of yourself and the person you fought hard to become.

Thirst Trap

Engineered to perfection, it's nearly impossible to look through various Instagram Models profiles without scratching your head or mumbling 'Damn!' to honor and acknowledge the beauty that exists around the world. Instagram Models, more than anybody else, have mastered what we call in the *Love in Hip Hop Era* the 'Thirst Trap' —known to most as a simple provocative image taken from various angles in locations such as the bed or the bathroom. The Thirst Trap intends to elicit likes, crazy emoji's, compliments, high praise, or words of obsessive thirst. While celebs like Nicki Minaj, Porsha Williams, and Amber Rose have recently refined and elevated the art of the thirst-trap photo, the concept has been out there on the internet ether for quite some time. In 2011, Urban Dictionary defined the thirst trap as 'any statement used to intentionally create attention or "thirst" and with the rise of visual social-media networks, the movement has reached new heights over past year or so.

What qualifies as a thirst trap? Anything that makes your temperature rise. Anything that makes you scratch your head and utter the words 'damn' while looking at your phone or your computer screen. Common thirst-trap genres include tatted up bodies, exposed torsos, twerking, cleavage, abdominals, pecs, nice backs, traps, and beautiful faces. These images — be it the V-shape of some guy's lower abs or a shot-from-above breast photo — excite and satisfy both the male and female. They serve as Fiji Water for the most dehydrated followers lurking on social media. Void of real love and affirmation in the *Love & Hip Hop Era* celebs and Instagram Models alike flourish with the attention gained while thirsty followers respond by sharing various displays of desperation (i.e.: 'Relationship Goals', 'Wifey', 'Marry me', and/or 'Follow me'.

3 Types of Thirst Traps:

1. **The Obvious Thirst Trap:** One doesn't need to look further than Kim Kardashian and her fully nude photo supported by two black lines with the caption 'I have nothing to wear. Lol.' The *Love & Hip Hop Era* has given way to the obvious thirst trap. Photos and other pictures such as the one I am referencing, shamelessly demand a response from its viewers. To any reasonable person, you know what the photo is for. Most times the person behind the photo openly admits its purpose either by hash tagging it #thirsttrap or by making it so overtly sexual there's no room for doubt or confusion. Women and men who are in search of any kind of attention they can get welcome the thirstiest comments from the thirstiest people. Lira Mercer aka Lira Galore is a good example, as are regularly free spirited Kathy Drayton and MizzTwerkSum.

2. **The Mendacious Thirst Trap:** This is the catch-you-off-guard photo. We call the sneaky thirst trap. It offers up the slightest pretexts, in order to convey that the person posting the pic isn't shopping for compliments, but will still welcome them when they occur. One example of the *Mendacious Thirst Trap* photo, is posting a photo of a Flat Tummy Tea packet that somehow manages to catch you at just the right angle to show off those yoga pants and hips followed by the hashtag #fitlife; or a photo of 'my new waist trainer.' This is really an opportunity to get a good selfie in there.

3. **The Disavowed Thirst Trap:** This is the most common of them all because it requires the least amount of effort. This person wants to seem totally unaware of the thirst they are sending (BREAKING NEWS: They are very aware of the thirst they are posting), and accompanies the pic with an alleged caption so ridiculously unrelated, so left field to avoid accusations of setting a thirst trap. A good example of this is when someone takes a topless selfie from their bed, casually showing off their breast and Tiffany and Co. necklace but captions the photo with the words of Dr. Martin Luther King Jr. *'Darkness cannot drive out*

darkness, only light can do that. Hate
cannot drive out hate. Only love can do
that.'

Because the *Love Factor* no longer exists we come up with various things to fill voids (such as the over-the-top selfie). The Love & Hip Hop Era gave way to the thirst trap which is perceived by some as nothing more than a sad, desperate play for validation; baiting those lurking on the internet into telling you you're pretty should never be an option. I mean, that's what you have best friends for, but when the love is gone and/or it no longer exists, we'd go just about anywhere to hear something nice…even from complete strangers.

However, there is no need to hate. Some individuals have built successful brands and followings through this method. For some, they now can provide for themselves and their family. To be honest, at least on a very small level, there is a certain kind of gratifying, superficial self-pleasure to be gained through perfecting a successful thirst trap. Instagram, which can easily be renamed, is basically one big Thirst Trap. Whenever we post there or on any other form of social media for that matter, we do it for some form of gratification.

Shack'n up

I remember living with my girl. I remember giving up my one bedroom apartment and trading my freedom, space, peace and serenity in to spend every day and night with my girl. I remember leaving it all behind. In all honesty, part of my independence felt like it was left in my one-bedroom apartment. But, it was the move that my girl and I felt was best at the time. I recall moving in with her. I arrived and began bringing what few things I had with me. I remember feeling like: '...Part of this is cool but part of this feels like I've abandoned everything I worked for. Nothing in this house feels like me. Nothing in this house is mine and nothing in this house has my name on it...not even the TV or this couch I'm sitting on.'

Not every guy is like me. I understand that. However, in the *Love & Hip Hop Era* we have a lot of men that want to mooch off and live off of women. We have a lot of men that don't want to work, refuse to work and would rather sit at home and play Madden and NBA 2K all day. I have always had my own. I have always provided for myself. So for me my time of shacking up (shack'n up) was not about being lazy. Shack'n up for me was not a time my ambition waivered. For me, shack'n up was a time to get right, save up and see if my girl was actually the one for me.

While living with my girl, my relationship with the Lord grew stronger. So, my walk with the Lord grew stronger. It didn't take long for me to know if she was the one or not. However, there was scripture that compelled me, along with the constant pressure from my spiritual coach, to ultimately make my way down the aisle…well to the court house in my case. See, it was one thing to shack up and not know better. But once I became aware, once I came into the light, I discovered that how I was living was in direct opposition to God's word. I was reminded in scripture that obedience is better than sacrifice. I have always known I was going places. I have always believed that I would make something of my life. I refused to let poverty or anything else hinder me or hold me down. However, there were some things I needed to change. There were some things I needed to do differently in order to align myself with God's vision and purpose for my life. I needed to, number one, get married. I needed to stop running away from a covenant union just to allow myself to be free and have the excuse to still see and entertain other women. For me, getting married helped bring order, focus and clarity to the rest of my life. When God cannot trust you, He cannot use you. The harvest is plenty but the laborers are few. I wanted and desired to be used by God therefore I had to first clean me up.

Shacking up, also known as cohabitation, cuts down on commitment. The message you send by shack'n up is: 'I'd really only like to take part of you. And maybe some time later I'd like to take all of you.' No wonder so many cohabitating couples break up or fall into unhealthy patterns. The relationship defines itself by a holding back of commitment.

People, more-so men who shack up with their girl, are less committed to that relationship but also less committed to future relationships. Also, cohabitating men who go on to marry are significantly less committed to the marriage itself than men who don't cohabit. Just so that we are clear, this is not *preacher talk* or a *holier-than-thou* stance. This is scientific with proven facts through research and data.

In the book, *The Ring Makes All the Difference: The Hidden Consequences of Cohabitation and the Strong Benefits of Marriage,* the author explores the many downsides of an increasingly popular practice among young couples that is especially prevalent with the Love & Hip Hop generation: living together before marriage.

We already know ideologically that marriage is a different relationship than shack'n up. Marriage is actually a very pro-woman institution. However, people don't fully realize what a raw deal for women shack'n up is. Women tend to bring more to the relationship— more work and more effort in tending to the relationship—but they get less satisfaction in terms of relational commitment and security. We sometimes think of marriage as a 'ball and chain' relationship. However, when two become one, they are—in a much healthier way—two independent individuals coming into the relationship, rather than the kind of unhealthy mishmash we find in shack'n up.

Some couples want to 'test drive' their relationship before committing to marriage just as you would before buying a new car. The question is: Does this help or hurt? Might living together give couples any good 'marriage practice' in some areas—like communication?

Actually, the data suggest that shack'n up train's couples to fight in an unhealthy toxic way. Because they don't have the commitment or security, couples who shack up tend to be more relationally and emotionally manipulative. One person may not have any intentions of leaving, but the other partner has the sense that he or she could leave. So, their interactions are different - the way they negotiate, the way they ask for things from one another.

One might ask are there any statistical upsides to shack'n up together? There's only one I've ever come across: 'elevated sexual encounters.' Couples who shack up are likely to have sex more often. But that's only early in the relationship. It doesn't maintain itself over time. Over the long haul, married couples have more sex and have more fulfilling sex.

Shack'n up and the impact on the kids

Real men salute the single mother that takes care and provides for herself and her kids. More importantly, real men respect the woman, the single mother, who does not bring various random men around her or her children. Many parents, single mothers in particular, are living life on their own terms in the *Love & Hip Hop*

Era. However, they fail to realize the damage they cause their children by exposing them to multiple men; running in and out of the house as well as in and out of their life.

What type of problems do children in cohabitating households tend to experience?

Safety is the absolute highest risk for kids. The risk for harm and abuse is three to four times higher for kids living with mom and her boyfriend. Researchers say that few things place children in more harm than having them live with an unrelated adult in the home.

Cohabitating homes hear more profanity and see significantly more drug use, more alcohol abuse, and more infidelity. The other surprising finding is that cohabitating couples earn dramatically less than their married peers. Even sadder is the fact they are also less likely to spend that money on the children.

What would you say to those who believe shack'n up and cohabitating can help people marry the 'right person'?

First of all, I am the first to acknowledge that l shacked up when I started out. However, the sooner young couples can understand that in most cases it doesn't end well, the better off they'll be. Young couples say to me and inbox me all the time, "You mean you don't want us to be soul mates?" I often times have to remind people, nobody marries his or her soul mate. You become soul mates by living life together through the years.

So often cohabiters are looking, in the first year, for what comes only after years— even decades! —of life together. You are setting yourself up for a drastic disappointment if you think life works that way.

Just as nobody buys a car without taking it for a test drive, most people—about two thirds of couples—don't get married any more until they've lived with their proposed lifetime partner. This has been true for a while, even though studies completed through the 2000s showed that couples who lived together first actually got divorced more often than those who didn't. But a spate of new studies looking at cohabitation are starting to refine those results.

A paper in the Journal of Marriage and Family presented to the Council on Contemporary Families says that past studies have overstated the risk of divorce for cohabiting couples. The important characteristic is not whether people lived together first, but how old they were when they decided to share a front door.

It turns out that shack'n up/cohabitation doesn't necessarily cause divorce and probably never did. Shack'n up is a problem because it is and has become the preferred permanent way of living for many young couples in the *Love & Hip Hop Era.* These couples have no intention of marriage. Some men lead women on causing them to believe that one day they will get married while he really never has intentions to put down the video games, work or get married. This denies good women the opportunity to engage with actual partners and relationships that actually want to do it right. What leads to divorce is when people move in with someone – with or without a marriage license – before they have the maturity and experience to choose compatible partners and to conduct themselves in ways that can sustain a long-term relationship.

So what's the magic age?

It is unwise to either move in or get married before the age of 23.

Other family experts say that's lowballing it. Economist Evelyn Lehrer (University of Illinois-Chicago) says the longer people wait past 23, the more likely a marriage is to stick. In fact, Lehrer's analysis of longitudinal data shows that for every year a woman waits to get married, right up until her early 30s, she reduces her chances of divorce. It's possible that a woman may also be reducing her chances of marriage, but Lehrer's research suggests later marriages, while less conventional may be more robust.

One of the reasons shack'n up was linked with divorce in prior years was that poorer people tended to move in together and then slide into marriage when they got pregnant. But their financial and economic circumstance did not improve. So it might not have been the shack'n up, but the poverty that was causing the split. Wealthier people tended to wait to get married.

The situation, today, has changed. 70% of all women aged 30 to 34 have lived with a boyfriend according to Kuperberg. Many of them are educated and wealthy. Sharon Sassler, a professor at Cornell who's writing a book on cohabitation, says that the amount of time a couple dates before moving in together is important. College educated women date guys for an average of 14 months before they become roomies. For non-college educated women, the waiting time is more like six months, because the lure of a single rent check is just too irresistible. Obviously, that situation is more prone to problems.

One of the biggest predictors of break-ups with couples of all types, is whether they have a child without meaning to. Sometimes an unintended or unexpected pregnancy is what pushes a couple to move in together or to marry.

What other factors predict a successful cohabitation-to-marriage journey? Coincidentally, in another paper released the same day, researchers at the University of Miami in Coral Gables found that there might be physical traits at work. Not surprisingly, more attractive people were more likely to get married than less attractive people. Not by much, and mostly that rule only applied to women.

Why get married at all? Why not just live together as long as it suits both parties?

Marriage has been shown to have a bunch of physical and health benefits that shack'n up has not yet been shown to have. Some experts believe it is because more unmarried cohabiting couples used to be among the less well off. But in a recent study of married and just-living-together couples, a researcher at the University of Virginia found that the brains of spouses responded differently to stress than the brains of living-together couples.

Are you single or dating someone you think may be the one? Or do you have kids who are dating and may be thinking wedding bells at some point?

If so, you may want to consider the importance of marrying before moving in together or of teaching your kids about the pitfalls of shacking up.

More and more couples are choosing to move in together before marriage. One reason is to save on rent. Yes, saving on rent. Saving on rent is not, and should not be, a reason to live with someone who may or may not become your spouse. In fact, it is a really bad reason.

Platonic Love

Platonic Love in the *Love & Hip Hop Era* reigns supreme. This is problematic for a lot reasons. By definition, platonic love in its modern popular sense is an affectionate relationship into which the sexual element does not enter, especially in cases where one might easily assume otherwise. A simple explanation of platonic relationships is a deep, non-sexual friendship between two heterosexual people of the opposite sex.

So just about everybody and they momma has that one friend that we call our 'best friend.' Typically our said 'best friend' knows our most sacred secrets, has been there for us through some of our most difficult times and is always the first person you call when you are having problems, such as a fight or an argument with your significant other. Might I add, the 'best friend' is often times very attractive and somebody you low key wouldn't mind being in a relationship with.

The Love & Hip Hop generation has taken platonic love to new heights. This generation has abandoned real relationships for over-hyped friendships…some of which come with benefits. Nobody is looking for love these days. Why? Because everybody has a *#MCM* or a *#WCW*. Everybody has a *bae* or *boo*. Everybody has a *side piece* or a *side chic*. And as a result, no one wants the real thing.

When I was in the game, I used this same method/tactic to avoid real commitment with women I was involved with romantically. I had tons of 'best friends' and I was the 'best friend' to tons of women. Not bragging by any means, but as I stated earlier…I was who I was and I am who I am and I'm cool with both people. Not proud nor shamed. Just at peace with who I was and who I am today.

The funny thing about being the 'best friend' is that other guys assume you are sexually involved with the girl they want so very badly. Then rumors start to fly;

'You know Chris hitting that right?" or "You know Sain smashing that, he got to be bro. She bad!" But the truth is, women have always confided in me. Girls have always confided in me. I remember as early as elementary school when girls would start asking me for male advice. Girls eventually turned into women and not very much has changed. To this day, I remain the one many of my female friends come to about their relationships. Some still want to know what my thoughts are on why their man is doing this or doing that or not doing this and not doing that. A default consequence associated with this place women have indirectly given me is the fact that there are a lot guys that do not like me or are intimidated or jealous of me simply because the women they love have placed me on a pedestal. The sad part is 98% of the guys don't know me. They have never seen me; they have never talked to me; but I am probably as real as they come. However, the mystique has been too much to overcome. It has been too much to bare. The rapper Nas said it best: 'Men fear what they don't understand, hate what they can't conquer, I guess it's just the theory of man.'

With all due respect to the topic at hand, I am a firm believer in platonic friendships especially when you are in a committed or serious relationship. This even includes marriages. When done right, with respect and integrity, the love and support of a close friend can be instrumental in helping one get through difficult or tough times and situations. When he or she respects your situation, whether it is a romantic relationship or marriage, and can provide insight, an unbiased viewpoint or unfiltered perspective, this can be healthy. Call me crazy, but those of us thriving and surviving in the *Love & Hip Hop Era* have bucked conventional wisdom and traditional norms. Not all I agree with, but when it comes to friendships, especially when you have real genuine friends, they should not be voided out of your life just because you got married. I believe this generation understands that.

Selfie Obsession

I have mixed feelings about the emergence of the 'selfie.' In full disclosure, I may be a low key hater of the individual selfie (selfies featuring myself only) because I have never personally been able to take a successful selfie. With that being said, shout out to those that have mastered the selfie and look good doing it. Keep on keeping on.

What I like about the selfie is the fact that it has resulted in a record number of people actually putting some time and effort into how they look. I see weaves done right. I see folk's make-up on point. I see edges laying down. I see brushed teeth and combed hair. I see effort. Most people that takes selfies, regardless if it took you 5,888 attempts to get that one, by the time it is posted on social media, whether it be Twitter, Facebook, Instagram or Snapchat, folk's be looking good. I will admit, there is one thing that grinds my gears more than anything else, one thing that irritates me more than anything else. It may seem random, but, it is the female who goes out in public with the too little scarf wrapped around her head with pajama pants on. Thanks to the selfie, at least via social media, those people don't exist. I guess I should cross my fingers but so far, I have never seen a female wearing the bandana scarf, the one that is matted down and smell like sleep, in a selfie.

What I dislike about the selfie is the fact that some females put more effort into getting the angle and filter right on their daily selfie than they do their actual relationship. *The Love & Hip Hop Era* has in a lot of ways, created this semi-narcissistic personality trait in people. Because the love factor is absent and because we no longer tell each other how much we love them and how much they mean to us, people have ventured out to receive the affirmation they so very badly desire by way of the selfie. Think about it, if your man would act right and was faithful and told you how beautiful you are then showed you how amazing you are, would there really be a need for a selfie? Unfortunately, that is not the case for over 85% of women in relationships. They have found creative ways (thirst trap, selfies, etc.) in the *Love & Hip Hop Era* to get what their heart desires; attention, affection and appreciation.

All in all, I am not mad at the selfie. I just have mixed feelings about the *Love & Hip Hop* generation's love affair with them. Although I suck at taking them, I love when my wife takes a selfie. She gets along with the camera very well, no filter needed. I love when she takes them and sends them to me while I am out impacting people. If nothing else, it serves as a reminder of what I have at home which makes me excited to get home because I know what is waiting for me. Pray for me. One day I will learn how to take a selfie.

Part 2

Diminished Social Skills:

The *Love & Hip Hop* generation has forgot about romance, the value of trust and intellectual conversation. Unfortunately, a strong text game is the new deep. For the life of me, I do not understand why people no longer talk about their issues. I do not understand why people don't verbally communicate with each other anymore. Most people today, will go to Facebook or Instagram to make a post about a person they use to text and talk to everyday now that they are having issues with one another. Communicate…even when it is uncomfortable or uneasy. One of the best ways to heal, is to simply get everything out.

A man's biggest mistake is giving another man the opportunity to make your woman smile, simply because you refused to communicate effectively. Often time's men and women, alike, shut down. They isolate themselves and go into this deep silence. When the lines of communication are not open, typically the number one thing that follows is some kind of split. Without the ability to communicate what do you have? The inability to effectively communicate is the next leading cause of break-ups and divorces after financial issues. This whole business about just randomly cutting people off unexpectedly is sad. Stop cutting people off with no warning and learn to communicate and resolve your issues with someone like an adult! The IDGAF mentally has crippled our ability to mend relationships and broken hearts. What is wrong with talking it out? Just because you have a fall out doesn't mean your friendship or relationship has to end forever.

If she stops asking questions and initiating conversations, you're no longer on her mind. Make no mistake about it, when she goes silent, you have become irrelevant. The worst thing you can do is listen to what she's been through then put her through it again. Being single is better than being lied to, cheated on and disrespected.

Nowadays you have couples that are in the same room and instead of having a conversation, you know, a real face-to-face conversation, where people are actually using real words, they choose to text each other. Simple exchanges sometimes turn into full blown disagreements and arguments because instead of actually talking you chose to text.

FUSS & FIGHT: ALL WE DO IS ARGUE

If all you do is argue, you are not in a healthy relationship. You are on a debate team. Real couples have mastered how to communicate, even during difficult times. Consistent arguing and disagreeing can create distance and discord in a relationship. Never push away the one who truly loves you to the point of no return. They may love hard, but are just as capable of letting go even harder. You are in a relationship to smile, to laugh, to be happy and make memories. You shouldn't constantly be arguing, upset and crying. However, sometimes you out grow people. Don't try to fix or repair, just accept it and move on. When the arguing reaches the point of disrespect, it may also be a sign to let go. Although you may love and care for one another, sometimes you have to try not to care, no matter how much you really do. Because, sometimes you can mean nothing to someone who means the world to you. At the end of the day, strive to be a man's peace and I guarantee he will always run towards you. Be a man's headache and no matter how much you bring to the table, he will hate being around you. Cut all that arguing out!

5 WAYS TO ATTRACT A MAN

I certainly cannot speak for all men, but if I must say so myself, I have done pretty good; When it comes to attracting a man, I have five things women can do to get the attention of the 'right one'.

1. **Ambition is Attractive:** Men are not only intrigued but extremely attracted to an ambitious woman. This is not to be confused with 'Ms. Independent' and 'Ms. I-Don't-Need-A-Man.' The way a man sees it is simple: Get up every day, handle your business, take care of your responsibility and look good doing it. Men love a woman that slays in all facets of her life.

2. **Have a life of your own:** In the Love & Hip Hop Era men do not give up or sacrifice their relationships with their best friends. Understand and respect that. Times have changed. In no way shape or form are his boys more important, but he values his friends and their time together. The best way to offset the feelings of neglect is to get you some friends. If you already have friends…even better. Call them. All of them. Hang out. Go out. Get sexy. Go to lunch, go have some drinks. Live a little…on your own terms, separate from your man. Give him a chance to miss you. You will be happy with

how excited he is to see you and to spend time with you.

3. **Be Fun to be around:** Most men love to kick it. Most men love to chill and have fun. The perfect complement to a man that operates this way is a woman who operates this way. Embrace NFL Sundays and all the games he and the fellas plan on watching while eating wings. In fact, put a smile on, something semi sexy even, you know, some sweats or something and make sure there is enough wings and slices of pizza for all the fellas over to the crib. We know you might not care about the game but live in the moment with the fellas. Turn up when they turn up…big plays during a game is something everybody can celebrate together. Even you!

4. **Know how to communicate:** Nothing is more attractive to a man than a woman who knows how to communicate. A woman that can articulate what it is she wants is a major turn-on to a man.

5. **Maintain Your Appearance:** It is evident and apparent to a man when a woman is intentional and consistently puts effort into her appearance. It is attractive to a man. A man, before anything else, is a visual person. A good personality is nice. A new car is even nice. But all of that is secondary to a man. What matters and what is as

important as having and maintaining a clean home is the woman who looks good, keeps her hair up, nails did and feet done.

5 WAYS TO KEEP YOUR MAN

It is important to first understand that a man that does not want to be kept won't be. Now that we have a mutual understanding, let me provide some specifics on the things you can do to keep your man.

1. **Provide a Challenge:** Men are competitive by nature. Most men welcome anything that sounds remotely close to a challenge. Be it basketball, cards, pool, video games etc. The same is also true when it comes to women. The 'Hard-to-Get' woman is the most coveted. The woman that can make a man work, the woman that can make a man put in some real effort, the woman that can provide a man challenge is the one most men find attractive. Be great every day. Real men appreciate it.

2. **Have a little edge about yourself:** Men like a woman with a little attitude. In this instance, attitude is not referring to the disrespectful type or the rude type. Attitude is more about the subtle confidence a woman possesses mixed with a little snazzy and a little jazzy. Be able to respectfully put a man in his place if need be or if necessary all while maintaining your lady-like. Be a queen at all times. Have a little edge about yourself.

3. **Be Supportive:** For a man in society, the hardest thing about success is finding someone that is genuinely happy for you. Like women, men need to be affirmed. Men need to be encouraged. Set out to be your man's biggest cheerleader. Desire to be his teammate. Not his opposition.

4. **Encourage Him:** Throughout the course of a day, the week, the month and the year, men very seldom hear anything good about their personhood. The last person he needs to hear something negative from is you. Every chance you get, encourage that man. Look for reasons to praise him. Even if he doesn't deserve it at that exact moment, make it a point to praise him, acknowledge him, and encourage him. Nine times out ten, he is fighting a battle you know nothing about.

5. **Enjoy each other:** Nothing makes a man more likely to stay, than a woman who he absolutely enjoys being around. What makes this thing unique is the woman who actually enjoys being with the man just as much. Sex is cool if that is what you both enjoy. A movie is cool if that is what you both enjoy. Dinner is cool if that is what you both enjoy. Going out (to the club) is

cool if that is what you both enjoy. Regardless of what it is, as long as you enjoy each other, you will never have to worry about the other person leaving.

3 TIPS FOR EMOTIONAL HEALING

In the *Love & Hip Hop Era*, people everywhere are struggling through life with damaged emotions and self-esteem. Many people have endured a lot of negative things that have caused untold damage that needs to be dealt with. But all too often, these hurts are simply hidden away or swept under the rug in an attempt to make it appear as if the hurt never happened. Through my own life experiences and setbacks and from several years of helping others through this process, I've discovered that although God wants to help those who really want emotional healing, there are some very important steps these individuals must take for themselves. If you want emotional healing, one of the first steps is facing the truth. You cannot be set free while living a lie. You can't pretend that certain negative things didn't happen to you.

I have come to realize that we have become experts at putting up walls and barriers and stashing things into the back of our minds, pretending they never happened. Why are we afraid to bring things into the light? The number one reason is because we are afraid of what other people will think us. We are afraid of being rejected, misunderstood, or unloved by those we care about. The greatest prison people live in is the fear of what other people think of them.

The next step toward emotional healing is acknowledging, then, confessing your faults. At some point, the right time will reveal itself to you and it will be an opportunity to share what you have been through, what you have overcame, with someone else. There is something liberating about verbalizing it to another person; it does wonders for us—but use wisdom. Not everybody cares, some are just curious. Make sure to choose someone you know you can trust. Be sure that by sharing your story with someone else, you don't simply transfer your burdens onto that individual's shoulders. Also, don't try to dig up old hurts and offenses that have been buried away and forgotten.

Turn your mess into a message. When I finally worked up the courage to share what I had survived in my life, I actually began to feel the weight be lifted from my heart and from my shoulders. The freedom I felt was an emotional reaction to the things I had kept buried inside of me for so long. Now, when I talk about my past and what I've been through, it's as though I'm talking about somebody else's life, not my own. See, I've been redeemed. I've been healed and restored and my past doesn't bother me anymore. In fact, I now use my experience to inspire other people.

Finally, you must assume some personal accountability and responsibility. Some people are caught in a matrix of denial, afraid of what might happen if others find out their truth. But as long as they deny the past and the things they've been through and overcame, they're never going to be free from it.

Nobody can be set free from a problem until they're willing to admit they have one. A gambler, drug addict or anyone who has lost control of their life will remain in bondage and will suffer until they're able to say, 'I need help because I've got a problem.'

Even though our problems may not have been our fault, we have no excuse for allowing the problem to manifest, grow and even take control over our entire life. The experiences and what we've been through in the past may have made us the way we are, *but we don't have to remain that way.* We can take back control by taking positive steps toward change. Whatever your problem may be, confront it head on, consider confiding in a trusted friend, and then admit it to yourself.

Confront your truth. It can be the beginning of your tomorrow!

THE TYPE OF WOMEN MEN LOVE

It is no secret that every woman loves a good man. What does a good man consist of? A couple points of emphasis to keep in mind, in my experience, women love an honest man. Keep it 100!

Women, of course, love different traits in a man but, some things they all have in common are the very things that aide in you changing her last name.

A woman loves a man that is proud to be with her, unafraid to show her off and openly displays his love for his woman in front of his boys and in front of his family. A woman loves a man that is not on the fence about being with her. There is something about certainty that brings a sense of security to a woman. A woman loves a good man that is willing to fight long and hard for the woman he loves and believes in. A woman loves a man who is vocal about his feelings; tell her you love her. Tell her why you are upset and make it right. Learn to share everything you are feeling.

Women love men who are gentlemen. How do we define a gentlemen you might ask? A gentlemen is not a man who says nice things to women. A gentleman is a man who says nice things and his actions backs up his words. A woman loves a man that keeps his word, loves the Lord, and is committed, consistent, compassionate, literate, concerned and connected. These are the attributes of a good man. I can, with about 99%

certainty guarantee that if you find a man that embodies any combination of the attributes I shared with you, he has the potential to be everything you have ever wanted in a man. Yes, we all know the occasional outlier but if you seek a man with the characteristics I have provided, you just might find your Adam. Why? Because unbeknownst to women, these are the things that you love that you sometimes have a hard time identifying, communicating and articulating.

Part 3

DON'T BE MAD AT LOVE

Don't be mad at love because your previous significant other did you wrong. Be mad at them. Move on and let somebody else love you. That is their loss, not yours.

We have all been there before…some of us will embarrassingly admit, that we have even been there more times than others. At one time or another, you have fallen head over heels for a guy who simply is not the one for you. No matter how much you try to ignore the many red flags and even blatantly obvious signs, you continue to talk to him, see him, and obsess over a man who is simply not obsessing over you. Clearly, he is not the man you were meant to be with, but right now, you are in love and can't nobody tell you anything. Your friends and family can't understand what we see in this man; he won't work, he won't cook, he won't clean and yet, you claim you are in love. He is negative, sometimes verbally abusive, lacks drive and ambition and although you notice these things, you are still in the relationship. At times, you just simply don't know why you are in this relationship, but yet he somehow sticks around much longer than you should allow him to. You are not alone. Many women are often times enamored with the idea of love and therefore become blinded by their own hopes and dreams for this man and his potential while ignoring how they are being treated and emotionally drained.

A man has done nothing for you until he has made you his wife. So stop idolizing boyfriends. Don't be embarrassed, be real! People can see that you are not truly happy in your relationship. Be willing to let go and move on if you need to. But just in case you are waiting on just one more red flag to show you what you probably already know is true about the man in your life, below are six red flags that indicate that your Mr. Right is in fact your Mr. Wrong:

Red Flag #1: It Seems Like You Irritate Him

Does it seem like you get on your man nerves? I mean this in the simplest way possible. How does he react towards you? Whether it is something big or small, is your man simply not nice to you? Remember, 'Love' is patient. 'Love' is kind. I can keep going about LOVE but you get my point. It doesn't matter if he volunteers at the Boys & Girls Club of America, prepares food for the homeless at the homeless shelter every week, mentors refugees, is an elder at church, and barbeque every time friends and family come over on the 4th of July. Good deeds mean nothing if that same level of love and compassion is not also shown toward you. How does he treat you? Does he try to humiliate you or embarrass you in front of others? Does he show little care and concern for your feelings or how his actions may impact you?

A man's success is measured by what his wife and children say about him. Accomplishments and what you do in the community mean nothing if you fail at home. Regardless of how 'awesome' a person may be to the outside world, if he is treating you like hell at home then what is the point of keeping him around? Far too often, women allow a person's image or persona to speak for them and not the actual actions demonstrated towards them. Take away how he treats anyone or anything else and start really thinking about how he treats you. If you feel bitter, resentment, confused, upset or sad, more than happy, you are not being treated as the Queen you are or with the respect that you deserve.

Red Flag #2: He Is Not That Into You or Things You Care About

Brains and beauty? It doesn't matter. Cool and chill? It doesn't matter. Charismatic, funny and like sports? It doesn't matter. This type of guy only pays attention to you at night and when he has free time. He has no desire to truly get to know you as an individual. This kind of man is easy to spot because he doesn't invest time in you or things that are of interest to you. Text messages usually result in a one-word response which is frustrating especially when your text message garnered more than a one-word answer. When communicating face-to-face, conversations are usually short, vague and driven by you. He never has anything to talk about. Remember this: you don't have to chase a man that truly wants to stay or be with you. We are not that deep! When people treat you like they don't care believe them…they don't.

Very short and almost distant; he makes it impossible to really get close to him or to get to know him beyond the surface level. Any real attempts made toward getting to know him further or even talking about your interests, are usually blown off. These type of traits are often used by men as a defense mechanism to either 1) not get too close to you or 2) not allow you to get too close to him. He keeps the lines of communication with you open as opposed to ignoring you altogether because he knows, at some point, he might want to become more serious with you. But for now, he is doing just enough to keep you right where he wants you should he decide he wants to take things further with you.

Real men do not hide things they are proud of. If he is not showing signs that he's into you, I hate to break it to you, but he's not. We are not that deep!

What I have described for you is the Playa type. How do I know? Because at one point, I use to be this type of guy. Lord forgive me. These types of guys like to keep their options open, you know like R&B sensation, Trey Songz, hit single 'Cake'. Yup, we like to have our cake and eat it too; all the while leaving women feeling confused and misused as well as vulnerable (I used to act this way but have since been delivered). If he was truly interested in getting to know you, he would make time to do just that. Men are persistent when they want something. Men like certain type of challenges. He would take the time and even sacrifice time in learning what motivates you, your interests, hobbies and things you like and don't like in a man. Holding a one-time conversation about your interest and what motivates you and never revisiting it, is not considered showing interest. Most women I know, when they are truly interested in a guy, they want to know all about him. You know, women care to know things like his middle name, his momma name, where he grew up at. It sometimes feel like an interrogation. Most likely you do know all of these things about him or have tried to learn them in one way or another. Why? Because you cared enough to want to know. So if a man is not showing signs that he is into you, 9 times out of 10, he is not and you should probably move on as well.

Red Flag #3: You Call Him First. He Never Calls You

Yes it is true, that women are persistent. Women get things done. Women make things happen. All of these things are true of women but don't get it twisted, men are persistent and get things done as well. We may not be as efficient as women are, but nevertheless we get things done. As a woman, do you find yourself always contacting him first? I mean either calling or texting him. It could be because you are curious to know how his day is going or what he's up to and what he might have a taste for dinner tonight. Either way, you can't help but to reach out to him. Although inconsistent, sometimes the communication is great and other times he seems occupied, distant and irritated by your call or text or just flat out busy. Trust me, regardless of how demanding his life is, when a man is interested he makes time to show you how interested he is. Men, believe it or not, know how to prioritize. My wife does not have to always call or text me because I try to be intentional about contacting her; sending her sweet nothings and other flattering messages throughout the day. The man who is meant for you, will do these things because he simply wants to and knows it the right thing to do. He wants to hear from you just as bad as you want to hear from him.

Red Flag #4: Your Girls Strongly Dislike Him.

When the energy is not right, the energy is not right. Trust his energy. Don't let it kill your vibe. Unfortunately your girls recognizes it before you do. If only you would've have listened to your girls, because this time they were not hating, they were telling you the truth.

Everybody is not hating. Some folks are telling the truth. From the moment he approached you and the moment your girl saw you fall for him, she knew immediately, that he simply was not right for you nor was he the one. Although you tried to justify to her and explain all of the great things he has done, deep down inside you knew your girl was right from the start. Boy oh boy…the things we do to act like we found the one.

Thank God for the female intuition. God gave you a super power. Sadly, not enough women use it, trust it. Rely on it. Fortunately, for women with good supports and positive friends and people in their life, it is easier for people that know you to see the situation a little more clearly than you can. The 50,000 foot view allows them to see the big picture, the exact things you don't want to see and the things you refuse to acknowledge. Though at the time it might seem like your girls are hating, more often than not, your friend is looking out for you and your best interest because they only want to see you happy. Now, go call that friend and apologize for calling them a hater.

Red Flag #5: He Is Elusive

If you chase after God like you chase after a man, He will send you a man you won't have to chase after.

Ladies, do you ever take a minute to pump your breaks and ask yourself, what the hell are you doing? If you ever found yourself acting like the CIA lurking on his Instagram page or stalking his Facebook page and the people, other females in particular who like his post, pause, regroup and gather yourself. These types of behaviors can be called many things but, for the sake of this book we are going to call this 'chasing.' There is no better feeling in the world than to be wanted; especially by someone you love or you want. Most people like to feel wanted, but there are certainly limits as to what is too much attention; especially when it is not being reciprocated. The man of your dreams should be just as obsessed over you as you are him. You shouldn't have to chase after him and he certainly shouldn't be eluding you.

Red Flag #6: You Can't Tell If He Loves You or Not

If a man loves you and really wants to be with you, you will know it. If you have to question it, let it go.

One minute you are considering spending the rest of your life with this man because he is saying and doing all of the right things, next thing you know you can't find him or catch him, because he is now all of a sudden Mr. Elusive. If he is not disappearing on you, he is mistreating you. No man should ever waste your time nor should you be questioning how he feels about you. He should make it obvious how he feels about you. A man's feelings and his intentions for you should be apparent. If he just wants to be friends he should say that; and if he wants to pursue a relationship with you he should show you. A man who has not made it clear what his intentions are for you, allows not only for speculation to set in but also for the door to be left open for another man to potentially be to you everything he was unwilling to be. Would a man who sees you as the woman he wants to spend the rest of his life with allow someone else that opportunity? Would a man who sees you as the woman of his dreams let you get away?

Unfortunately in the Love & Hip Hop Era, a time where people live out their lives and relationships on social media, getting to know someone has become more difficult than ever before. Nowadays, it is easy to confuse who a person truly is in real life with who they want others to believe they are based on how they are online. Even scarier, is how easy it has become for women to feel a connection with a man that you feel you know based on their social media presence or similar interests. Please remember, a person's social media post does not equate to that being who they really are. And likes on your pictures don't always mean they are interested in you. If your 'Romeo' isn't exactly who you perceived him to be, and you know he isn't the one for you, stop wasting time hoping he starts treating you how you think he treats everyone else.

When your Adam shows up and enters your life, you won't have to question or doubt his true intentions with you. You will know he is right for you because your heart will confirm it and you will feel it. No man is perfect, but you certainly won't have any doubts about how he feels for you or how you feel about him. You deserve to be loved fully; by yourself and by the man of your dreams. So until your Adam crosses your path, ditch Mr. Elusive so he's not standing in the way. Fill your time only with those that are deserving of it. Your King won't show up until you remove the Joker.

Ambition is Attractive

The Love & Hip Hop Era has given rise to the man that embraces the independent woman. The Love & Hip Hop Era has also given rise to the man who no longer fears or is intimidated by a woman who is as equally successful or more and no longer does the man feel inadequate and less of a man if his female counter part makes more money than him. With that being said, it is important to understand, that not all men fit this mode. Yes, you still have the man of old, we've all encountered them, you know, the man who despises successful, ambitious women. And yes, the man who is lazy and desires to solely live off of his woman does indeed still exist. Just know, that the man who appreciates your efforts, who appreciates your success and accomplishments are on the rise.

In spite of how much a woman's ambition intrigues a man, ambition has, at times, come at a severe cost for some women. I think that women who are extremely driven to success, the ambitious type, get deterred. They get to a point in their lives where they are like, 'Oh shoot!' I am now 35 years old, and I still don't have a husband. I don't even have children yet and what does that say about me?' I think what it says is: Stay on the course because it's going to happen when it's supposed to happen. Don't force. Don't let momma or society speed up what God has already prepared for you. Let me remind you, it doesn't happen for everyone at the same time, so you can't compare your life to someone else's. Run YOUR race!

As real men, those of us that exist, we encourage you to keep grinding. Don't stop hustling and operating in your purpose. However, I like to challenge women I talk to about this topic to maintain an open heart and an open mind. Allow yourself to be vulnerable enough to embrace a child and to accept a child if and when it comes. The rub is this; The more success you have as a woman, that ultra-independence kicks in, the superhero in you is activated and you kind of start to internalize and believe, 'Well, I don't really need a man 'cause look: I have done-this-and-that and I have everything I want and need.' But that is a lie! One in which too many women believe and run with and end up lonely throughout their 30's and 40's. The truth is you do need a partner, you do need someone to love and someone that loves you back because at some point in your life you are not going to want to go through life alone and by yourself.

The *Love & Hip Hop Era* has birthed more ambitious women than any other era. Look around, check your newsfeed, look at your Instagram and witness the women in charge and doing their thing. It's encouraging to say the least. Educated professional and corporate women are often praised for their ability to run a successful business or climb the corporate ladder, but are hardly recognized or praised for their ability to remain focused and locked-in during the time it took to reach a certain level of success. When it comes to ambitious women, many people see the end result but very few consider the journey. At times, the level of focus needed to achieve success might also include sacrifices and placing a few things on the backburner (i.e. holding off on marriage or starting a family until later). Unfortunately, when a 30-plus year old woman is accomplished yet single, people will use the very thing they praised her for, against her. Her ambition, her persistence and resilience to ensure success and something to fall back on in case a good man never emerges all seems to backfire. The double-standard is still alive and well. A successful well-to-do male CEO of a well-known corporation in his late 30's early 40's might be regarded as one of the 'youngest in his position,' and no one says a word if he has no kids and has not got married yet. But for a woman with the same stat line, although she'd get praised and hi-fived on the work accomplishments, she'd be pretty much written off as too old to marry and too old to have kids. It's safe to say and assume that this very real dynamic is where the perception of having a 'biological clock' that's ticking sets in for the ambitious woman.

Sex over Commitment

A Guide to help you find your Adam

In the *Love & Hip Hop Era*, I have noticed that women fall in love similar to how people begin life — naive and full of optimism. Like many women around the world, you have experienced certain romantic issues that jaded your perception of relationships. I call these embodiments of romantic misfortunes the <u>Five Types of Guys to Avoid</u>. Unknowingly, the men of your past have paved the road to love and self-awareness in disappointment, tears, frustration and heartache.

1. **Mr. Sliced Bread:** This guy always wants the girl who is 'That Deal' right now. He will make you feel incredibly special, until, of course, your moment is over.

2. **Mr. Negativity:** This guy has deeply embedded issues. However, instead of seeking help and working through them, he attempts to chip away at your confidence. Mr. Negativity will start off strong. Although negative at his core, in the beginning, he will give extreme compliments and say all the right things to build you up in hopes of you letting your guard down. Then one day, his glass half empty perspective will spew nothing but toxic poison and negativity. You will notice his comments are more critical than affirming, more insulting than uplifting.

3. **Mr. Cuffing Season:** You think you two really have something special… until Cuffing Season is over and Sun Dress Season emerges. All of a sudden you see him entertaining other women or even going as far as buying gifts for another woman, something he certainly didn't do when you two were an item. Mr. Cuffing Season never sees a future with you, or any woman for that matter. He is seasonal. He gets some kind of arousal from leading women on during certain times of the year.

4. **Mr. Hot'n Ready:** This is the guy you settle for to prove something to all the other guys who dropped you like a bad habit. He likes the fact you have curves or a nice booty, a nice chest, things like that. Mr. Hot'n Ready is into you for a surface level and superficial reason, but you don't care because you are trying to stunt on your exes and you don't want to be alone. Unlike the men of your past, you are aware he is wrong from jump. However, his persistence to be with you soothes your damaged ego.

5. **Mr. Frito Lay:** This guy cannot fathom seeing himself being with one woman and doesn't understand how other men do it. He sees monogamy as selling out and as a reason to turn in his Playa Card, therefore he welcomes you and as many other women he can get, with open arms… Like Lays Potato Chips, you can't eat just one. Mr. Frito Lay appeals to you because

your relationship is open and you are still free to see other guys. However, it is through him that you learn you are just another chic on his roster.

The Common Thread: You

For some women, their past adventures, while hurtful, made it impossible for them to exist in their own madness. From being lied to, to being cheated on, their past relationships were anything but 'romantic.' However, it isn't until women consider the common thread in all their past escapades that they are able to check their emotional luggage. Have you ever noticed or considered, that the only thing all of your 'Mr. Wrongs' had in common was YOU?

It was you who granted these men access through your involvement with them. As women, you often times overlook the power you have in all our romantic pursuits. As women, you teach your possible suitors how to treat you. It is only when you truly examine your role in your romantic mishmash, that you discover that you are the common thread in all of your past relationships.

Like countless other women, because your best self was missing, you failed to attract a man worthy of you. And although, it is never solely about finding a partner who appreciates you; it is about appreciating and valuing yourself first, above all else.

Don't Settle for Less: Single Life

Almost seemingly out of nowhere, being single has all of a sudden become a bad thing. It is almost seen as if something is wrong with you, if you are single. There is no consideration given whatsoever to facts such as: you are single by choice or you want to get to know yourself better or you are working on loving you better so that someone else can also love you. I am here to put that nonsense to rest. Maybe I don't speak for everybody when I say this, but being single is not a bad thing. In fact, being single is better than being lied to, cheated on and disrespected.

Ladies, I will even take it a step further. Someday you will find someone that makes you feel like the wait was worth it and you will be happy it did not work out with anyone else. It is better to be single with standards, than to be in a relationship settling for less.

Part of the reason women settle for the wrong relationship with men is because they don't have the right relationship with self. Some women think that holding on makes you stronger, but sometimes letting go reveals your real strength. Stop giving certain people second, third and fourth chances when there are others still waiting for their first chance. Don't be fooled, men love a challenge until the challenge is to be faithful to one woman.

The *Love & Hip Hop Era* has made it socially acceptable to cheat on your significant other. In some outlandish and foolish way, this type of behavior by both men and women, has become the norm. However, let me remind you, you don't cheat on someone you love. You may be tempted, but as far as letting your flesh get so weak that you go all the way and give into temptation, it shouldn't happen. Cheating isn't always kissing, touching and flirting. If you have to delete text messages so that your partner does not see them, that counts to.

The Numbers

Forty-two percent of U.S. black women have never been married. Double that number for white women who've never tied the knot.

For starters, there are 1.8 million more black women than black men. So even if every black man in America married a black woman today, one (1) out of twelve (12) black women still wouldn't make it down the aisle if their hope was to marry a black man.

Achievement matters and so does credentials. Let's take 100 black men for example. By the time you eliminate those without a high school diploma (21 percent), the unemployed (17 percent) and those ages 25-34 who are incarcerated (8 percent), you have approximately a little over half of black men, 54 percent, whom many black women would even find acceptable.

The R&B group Destiny Child set man back 20 years with their hit song 'Soldier.' The lyrics went on to say 'If your status ain't hood, I ain't checking for you. You gotta be street if you looking for me…' Within a matter of weeks, lames became gangsters and cornballs picked up the bag. Every man became a goon or a thug after that record hit the charts. However, in spite of this tragic setback, there are still a lot of good men out there who are being overlooked. There are many women, who are trying to match up their education level and/or their corporate status to find somebody on the same level, but they are having trouble. That has nothing to do with manhood at all.

The consensus among many black women is that their preference is to marry a black man. And it's not that they can't find one to date. The issue, in many cases, is exclusivity.

You meet these great guys, you have a good relationship, and then it is like, 'I'm going to keep you around, and hopefully when I am ready to settle down, you'll be there. In full disclosure, I did something very similar and simply got lucky. My wife and I have been married for over five years but I definitely left everything to chance. Lucky for me, she was still there.

Men Where Are You:

The more I hear women's concerns about not being able to find decent men, the more my heart and mind becomes weary. The words of some of today's women leave me saddened and temporarily disheartened. However, I remain committed.

Some women blame the fact that they are single solely on men, insinuating that good men are rare and hard to find, that there are very few decent single men than ever before in history. This is not based on any verified data (which is always confusing anyway) but, there are also quality single men who cannot find the 'abundance' of quality single women relationship magazines always talk about.

Some black women say that 'most' black men are in prison, that 'more' black men are gay and that the 'best' black men are married to white women, but none of that has been statistically supported.

Although it is sad that there are many black men dying from gang violence and from drugs, that is not 'most' of the black male population. There are droves of black men who live beyond all of the things that are horribly wrong; and a great number of them are neither gay nor with white women.

The risky proposition is when women say that black men are beneath their level (financial or education), when in fact, black people in America don't yet have an intrinsic level. Even many of our so-called middle class counterparts live one paycheck away from disaster.

Ladies, if you examine a man's character first, you will find that there are more of us than you imagined.

Certainly men in America have challenges, but in this nation, we are both challenged, both male and female.

Even with all of our challenges, some of us are still finding each other and marrying each other. Anyone can point out that marriages are fewer and divorces are more abundant, but those are stats for the masses. They don't have to apply to the individual.

Perhaps the bigger problem is that many women are no longer in circles where quality black men can be found. Typically, once you graduate from college, it is over as far as having access to a social circle filled with potential partners. The sad fact is that many of us work in a world where there are few of us. We also live on a block where there are few of us, yet we complain about not finding us and talk about the sorry state of those of us we run into.

In the *Love & Hip Hop Era*, communities are fragmented, clubs are toxic and many church singles ministries misguide people into relationships with other people who attend church service, but do little to follow the Word of God. Yes, things are more difficult than they have been in a long time, but the difficulties appear even greater because of the way men, especially black men, are perpetuated. There are also countless negative misconceptions about men. Add the negative things being said about black men on television, in magazines, on WorldStar Hip-Hop and at the beauty salon by our fellow single black women. And one can't help but to conclude that it's all bad!

Hurt people, hurt people. I get it. I know why women say some of the vicious things that they say about men. It's because they are hurt and afraid. They are broken and broken people can't repair broken people.

Men are also hurt and afraid. Those of us over the age of 25 have a thought-provoking fear, which can sometimes lead us away from finding real love. The many temptations of the world are sometimes too much to overcome. Some have embraced what is now considered the accepted norm, which is to cheat, lie and have multiple partners that know about each other while others still hold out hope for the real, old fashion, unconditional love between one man and one woman.

Too many of us thought that we could do it on our own, that we could make things better for ourselves as individuals, but now, the seeds that were planted have blossomed, and we now realize that the harvest is plentiful, but the laborers are few and many of us cannot find a compatible mate.

Men and women fell from grace when we forgot how to communicate; stopped talking to each other and began talking about each other. If we wish to make things better, I believe it begins with communication and not via text message. The charge for both men and women is to begin to discuss the problems we both face, without expressing the fear and hatred that we have been spewing at each other.

I have one request that I wish would travel around the world faster than a TMZ story or a viral Facebook post. I want every person that reads this book to share it with another person, whether married or single. That one simple request is for men and women to begin to change our disposition about each other. Perception for some, is reality and we must begin to perceive each other differently so that we can love each other correctly.

I want to reiterate and let all women know that there are still some good, kind and decent men in the *Love & Hip Hop Era* although we are having a hard time finding all of them. Men are at the supermarket because we have to eat. Men are at the train station, because we have to commute to work, and yes, some of us can be found in worship, trying to get right with the Lord. Men are also at red carpet events, plays, museums, the library and the gym. Men can be found in a number of places and many times we are right beside you. All you have to do is look approachable. Try smiling, for instance. Be nice and open and you may get more than just a jive turkey recklessly asking for your number. Whatever you do, be grounded and inviting.

I suggest that both men and women to look for common things that exists in each other. If you are a single woman looking for a single man, look for examples of what you want in the men around you. Some man in your midst may be your reference point. Your father, brother, uncle, cousin or neighbor may be married and may serve as a good measurement for the men you date.

We may not look like your ideal man or come with the attributes and physical features you have down on your list, but many of us are hardworking, decent men with solid husband and father potential; ready to love and to be loved by you. You have to look around you and find real examples, because once you are convinced that we don't exist, (because perception is often times reality for some people) we all of a sudden, don't exist.

Women, stop saying that you can't find a good man, or that we just don't exist. Come at us in love and what you will find from many of the sane, single men is real love. We're trying to find you and we want you, too.

Where are the men? We're right here.

SELF LOVE

Self-love refers to the act of valuing one's own happiness and well-being. Self-love is a kind of acceptance that can be described as an unconditional sense of support and caring and a core of compassion for the self. It might also be considered a willingness to meet personal needs, allow non-judgmental thinking, and view the self as essentially worthy, good, valuable, and deserving of happiness.

Those who find it challenging to practice self-love or have barriers that make it difficult for them to experience compassion or love for themselves may find the support of a therapist or other mental health professional to be beneficial as they explore the reasons behind these difficulties.

Why Is Self-Love Important?

Self-love is considered to be an important component of self-esteem and overall well-being. It is generally difficult, if not impossible, to feel content without first being able to love and accept the self. Researchers have discovered that the practice of self-love is associated with a multitude of benefits, such as greater life satisfaction, increased happiness, and greater resilience.

People with high levels of self-compassion have been shown to often be able to overcome difficult life events, such as divorce, with more ease than those who are harder on themselves. The ability to affirm oneself has also been associated with improved problem-solving abilities and decreased procrastination, because it can help individuals recognize the effects of negative habits and behaviors (such as procrastination) without leading to a thought pattern that is excessively negative.

The risk of developing mental health issues such as depression, anxiety, and perfectionism can also be decreased through the practice of self-love. The practice of self-love can increase one's optimism and may be helpful for stress reduction, especially in the face of various life challenges.

Self-love can also lead to improved relationships. The idea that a person should practice self-love before attempting to pursue the love of others is one that is accepted by many, and research has shown that practicing self-love and self-compassion is likely to improve well-being in the context of interpersonal relationships. People who have self-compassion and practice self-love generally report feeling happier and more authentic in their relationships, and thus, they may be better able to assert their needs and opinions. Further, those who practice kindness and compassion on a personal level first, may be better able to show kindness and compassion to others and are generally more likely to do so. The ability to care for and love one's self generally indicates that one will experience a greater capacity to love and care for others.

It is generally considered to be normal for people to have periods in which they feel better about themselves and periods in which confidence and self-esteem wane. After failing at an important task, for example, one may question personal ability and self-worth. Self-love is considered to be an ongoing act, rather than a constant state. For many people, it takes effort, attention, and mindful attempts to practice self-compassion and affirm and accept oneself.

Can Self-Love Be a Bad Thing?

Self-love, in this context, can be said to differ from narcissism, as self-love is largely considered to be positive. Self-love is generally beneficial to happiness and well-being, and those who are encouraged to practice self-love may be more likely to achieve and experience success. While narcissism may sometimes be referred to as self-love, narcissism can more accurately be described as an excessive self-interest, combined with a general disregard of others and a lack of empathy.

In excess, self-love may become self-centeredness. A high level of fragile or shallow self-esteem, which may be facilitated by empty praises of well-meaning parents, teachers, or other caregivers during one's childhood, can lead individuals, especially adolescents, to develop traits of narcissism. Research has also shown that inflated self-esteem, which can be linked to excessive self-love, is often associated with cynicism, a lack of motivation, verbal defensiveness, and, in some cases, aggression.

Self-Love in Therapy

Certain distorted thought processes may make the practice of self-love difficult. Some individuals may believe that they are unworthy of love due to a lack of success in their chosen professional field, or because of certain personal characteristics that they perceive to be negative or flawed. Trouble with relationships or friendships may also lead some to feel as if they may never experience close friendship or love. This can contribute to spiraling negative thoughts that may also have a negative effect on the ability to love self. Often, cognitive and brief therapies prove helpful, as they focus on correcting these thoughts in order to improve one's ability to love oneself and develop greater self-compassion.

Early experiences such as trauma, abandonment, or neglect can also cause people to feel as if they are unworthy of love. Therapy can help people uncover possible reasons that it may be difficult to practice self-love. In therapy, people seeking treatment may become better able to understand the ways that early experiences still affect them and, with the help of a therapist, may be able to overcome past trauma and any feelings of self-loathing.

Therapy can also provide a space where one feels loved and accepted. The concept of unconditional positive regard, initially developed by Carl Rogers and used in person-centered (Rogerian) therapy, holds that providing a relationship in which one is truly accepted, without any conditions or judgment, allows healing to occur, in most cases. By providing unconditional positive regard, a therapist can also help people in therapy to learn to harbor that degree of love and acceptance toward themselves. For individuals who have never experienced love or acceptance and find it difficult to practice self-love as a result, this therapeutic bond may foster the development of self-compassion and love, leading to a state of improved mental health.

Cultural Differences of Self-Love

The expression of self-love can change depending on cultural context. Although self-love appears to represent an important aspect of human existence, people from some cultures may be less likely to speak positively about themselves. To others in spheres outside those of close friends and family, as in these cultures, modesty and humility may be more valued. One study found that although people from some East Asian cultures were found to love and feel as good about themselves as did the Americans also surveyed, those from East Asian cultures evaluated themselves less positively on a cognitive level.

Seven Ingredients for Self-Love

Self-love is a popular term today in the *Love & Hip Hop Era* that gets tossed around in everyday conversation. 'You have to love yourself more.' 'Why don't you love yourself?' 'If you only loved yourself, this wouldn't have happened to you.' 'You can't love another person until you love yourself first.' These are just a few of the self-love directives that we give or suggest as a way to living a more fulfilling life.

Self-love is important to our well-being. It influences who we choose for a mate, the image you project in public, and how you deal with the problems in your life. It is so important to your welfare that I want you to know how to bring more of it into your life.

The question, then, is: 'What is self-love?' Is it something you can buy? Can you get more of it by reading something motivational? Or, can a new relationship make you love yourself more? The answer to all of these questions is a resounding 'No!' Although they feel good and are gratifying, you can't grow in self-love through superficial activities because self-love is not simply a state of feeling good.

Self-love is a state of acceptance and appreciation for oneself that grows from actions that support our physical, psychological and spiritual growth. Self-love is dynamic; it grows by actions that mature us. When we act in ways that expand self-love in us, we begin to better accept our weaknesses as well as our strengths. There is less need to explain away our short-comings. We have compassion for ourselves as human beings struggling to find personal meaning, and are more centered in our life's purpose and values. We also expect to find fulfillment through our own efforts.

Here are my Seven Ingredients for Self-Love:

Ingredient 1: Become mindful. People who have more self-love tend to know what they think, feel and want. They are mindful of who they are and act on this knowledge, rather than on what others want for them.

Ingredient 2: Act on what you need rather than what you want. You love yourself when you can turn away from something that feels good and exciting to what you need to stay strong, centered, and moving forward in your life. By staying focused on what you need, you turn away from automatic behavior patterns that get you into trouble, keep you stuck in the past, and lessen self-love.

Ingredient 3: Practice good self-care. You will love yourself more, when you take better care of your basic needs. People high in self-love nourish themselves daily through healthy activities, like sound nutrition, exercise, proper sleep, intimacy and healthy social interactions.

Ingredient 4: Set boundaries. You'll love yourself more when you set limits or respectfully say no to work, love, or activities that deplete or harm you physically, emotionally and spiritually, or express poorly who you are.

Ingredient 5: Guard your heart. Bring the right people into your circle. The *Love & Hip Hop Era* has seen more frenemies than real friends. Frenemies describes so well the type of 'friends' who take pleasure in your pain and loss rather than in your happiness and success. My suggestion to you here is: Get rid of them! There isn't enough time in your life to waste on people who want don't want to see you shine. When you genuinely love yourself and your life, you will love and respect yourself more.

Ingredient 6: Forgive yourself. We humans can be so hard on ourselves. The downside of taking responsibility for our actions is punishing ourselves too much for mistakes in learning and growing. You have to accept your humanness (the fact that you are not perfect), before you can truly love yourself. Practice being less hard on yourself when you make a mistake. Remember, there are no failures if you have learned and grown from your mistakes; there are only lessons learned.

Ingredient 7: Live intentionally. You will accept and love yourself more, no matter what is happening in your life, when you live with purpose and design. Your purpose doesn't have to be crystal clear to you. If your intention is to live a meaningful and healthy life, you will make decisions that support this intention, and feel good about yourself when you succeed in this purpose. You will love yourself more if you see yourself accomplishing what you set out to do. You need to establish your living intentions, to do this.

If you choose just one or two of these self-love ingredients to work on, you will begin to accept and love yourself more. Just imagine how much you'll appreciate you when you exercise all seven steps to self-love. It is true that you can only love a person as much as you love yourself. If you exercise all of the actions of self-love that I describe here, you will allow and encourage others to express themselves in the same way. The more self-love you have for yourself, the better prepared you are for healthy relating. Even more, you will start to attract people and circumstances to you that support your well-being.

Part 4

Love & Hip Hop

Many have walked away from God looking for love. The pursuit of true love requires patience.

In the Love & Hip Hop Era, this generation does not like love. They like the idea of love. They like that little heart-drop flirty feeling you get when you are with that special somebody. They do not love love for real. See, love is sacrificial, love is tenacious it is not emotive. Our culture does not love love. The hip hop generation wants the emotion without laboring for the real thing.

By far, the worst thing you can do to yourself, is remain in an abusive and toxic relationship hoping that after each "Baby I'm sorry", things will get better. If you keep telling yourself, "I'll be able to work with him. He just needs more time", you are continuing a self-destructive cycle as well as lying to yourself. What does he need more time for? Does he need more time to see how awesome of a woman you are? Does he need more time to realize he treats you like crap and it is not right? Stop making excuses for him. You cannot keep staying, hoping that he will change his ways because until you leave, he will never change. A man only changes when he chooses to change. You will end up wasting valuable years of your life on a relationship that was not worth your love.

You have stayed too long in a relationship that is not making you happy. You have completely lost the essence of what true love and real love are supposed to be and what it is supposed to feel like. And in the process you have lost yourself trying to make things work. You have lost your dignity and your self-worth breaking your neck to please someone who does not appreciate anything you do. If being happy is the goal, how much more time are you going to waste trying to 'be happy'?

If it's broke, don't fix it. Know when to move on. Stop trying to put what is broken back together again. When you keep trying to piece a broken relationship back together time and time again, trying to get things back to how they use to be, typically you ruin the relationship for good. Pray and ask for discernment because at some point you have to know when it is time to let go. Sometimes, it is not because you want to, but because it is the only way you will ever be able to move forward with your life. Sometimes, the fact of the matter is that certain things are just not simply meant to be.

You deserve somebody that refuses to quit and that keeps fighting for you and with you no matter how hard things gets. Someone that consistently uplifts you and shows you a deeper connection than you have ever felt before. Someone that does not try to change you but instead chooses to help you grow. They motivate you to be better and demonstrate to you how dedicated they are to seeing you succeed. Believe it or not, but that is the type of love you deserve and will one day have. Get ready. The one for you is en route.

You were loyal, honest, committed, and faithful, caring and he still found a way to cheat. So explain to me why you're still crying over a man that clearly never saw your worth.

Your love is not a drive-thru. He can't keep coming in and out of your life as he pleases. Set boundaries. The boundaries that you set should not be crossed and playing with your emotions is one way to cross them. Real men know what they want so if he cannot decide what he wants, it is time for you to send him packing. You should not let anybody waste time by playing with your heart simply because they are unsure how they feel about you.

No matter who you are, somebody will hurt you physically and emotionally at least once in your lifetime. That person will be careless with your heart and reckless with your love. They will rip your heart into shreds and have absolutely no clue of all the pain it has caused you. You will feel beat down and broken and as though the pain and hurt will never end. But, through it all, even when you think you have reached your breaking point, you will realize how truly strong you are for all you have endured. Like no other time in your life, you will understand what self-love is and what it is all about. You will develop a new appreciation for yourself and in due time, you will be made new. You will reflect back on the moments that brought you your greatest hurt, and you will shake your head with a mysterious grin at who you used to be. You will be stronger and wiser than ever and nothing that tries to hinder you or cause you harm will prosper. Be grateful but more importantly be proud of all you have survived.

Have you ever wondered why you keep attracting the wrong type of men? Could it be that every time the men you go for do something wrong, you ignore it and make excuses for him? You tell yourself lie after lie and then convince yourself that you are wrong instead of following your intuition. Every time he comes back around, showing interest in you, he wins back your heart and you go right back to what was already deemed 'no good' for you. It might be time to start listening to your heart and make a decision to move on.

Men know…within 3 months if you are the one or not

Depending on who you ask, you are likely to receive a variety of answers. Why? Because all men are not the same. Answers to what, one might ask…The answer to "When do men know if you are the one?"

Known as somewhat of a female connoisseur; during the years I was in the game, dating multiple women, I always took the time to ask myself, 'was this one or that one the actual one?' To be fully transparent about whether or not I knew if a female was the one, I can honestly say that after about 90 days I kind of had an idea.

Some call it discernment. Regardless, I believe that as men, we know. The one thing that made getting married for me so difficult at the time, especially living and operating in the *Love & Hip Hop* Era, was the fact that over the years I had accumulated what I would call and consider quality women. You know, the type I could possibly marry.

Yes, I am 100% certain that I made the right choice and that my wife was specifically created for me. However, as a man who is as real as they come, I also have to admit that along my journey, I met some women that had the potential to have my last name. I guess the best and safest way to say it is: "You just know."

Now, as men, do we prolong the situation or draw out the process. Absolutely. See, 90 days is the benchmark to make sure we are sure. Three months is to make sure we are certain. But to be real, something deep down in our gut, something in our spirit tells us she is the one well before 90 days. As men, we are often afraid of rejection. We are often afraid of failed relationships, so the 90-day benchmark serves as a barometer to see whether or not any pertinent issues will arise and if there is anything that takes place during that time that indicates or reveals to us she is not the one.

Before I decided that it was time to get married, I opted to be engaged for 12 months. In some ways I was prolonging the inevitable but in some ways I needed the extra time to get my mind right. See, I knew she (my wife) was the one, but I first had to deal with my own issues. I had several women prior to her and it was imperative that I closed those chapters. By closing those chapters, I mean, it was important enough to me, to bring closure to our relationships. Why? Because I've always had meaningful relationships with the women I dealt with.

When you add the 12 month engagement to my overall time table, I dated my wife for nearly six years. Nearly six whole years I was able to buy time and put off marriage. Remember, as men we know. We know within three months whether you are the one or not. I could no longer keep up my ways. I knew. As the old saying goes, "When you know better, you do better."

I started to feel selfish. My wife, then girlfriend/fiancé, was deserving of a ring. She was deserving of a wedding. She was deserving of my last name. She was ready; she had been ready but patiently waited and gave me the time I needed and the time I asked for to prepare myself to spend the rest of our lives together. I knew she was the one. I knew within 90 days. I managed to go six years avoiding what I knew in 60 days. Selfish!

Cheaters: Games they Play

You don't cheat on someone you love. You may be tempted, but as far as letting your flesh get so weak that you go all the way and give into temptation, it shouldn't happen. Cheating isn't always kissing, touching and flirting. If you have to delete text messages so that your partner does not see them, that counts to. The sad thing about cheating is that it is often times premeditated. One has already made up in their mind they are going to step-out on their significant other. Cheating was in the mind long before it actually happens in the physical.

Cheating is defined in the clinical world as 'anything that takes emotional energy away from your relationship'. So for instance, if you are thinking about your ex when you should be getting dressed for the company's Christmas Party dinner that would be an example. Or, if you are lurking on someone whom you find attractive Instagram page and you are having thoughts of being with that person or talking with that person and it causes you to unconsciously be short with your significant other, again, that is an example of cheating. When you take emotional energy away from your current relationship, this is a form of cheating. Most people do not know and/or understand this concept. I recommend that in general, people in relationships and marriage couples, ask for forgiveness daily for both seen and unseen sins you have either intentionally or unintentionally committed.

You don't have to cheat to lose your girl or your woman. You can lose her from lack of communication, attention and lack of respect. It's not all about what you do, sometimes it's about what you don't do. I often remind men and women of this when turmoil has seem to hit their relationships. Sometimes what we don't do in a relationship causes and creates the biggest voids with our significant other. In many cases, a good woman is willing to fight long and hard for the man she loves and believes in, but just because she is willing to fight for you, does not mean she won't leave you if you take her love and loyalty for granted.

Love is a two way street. It requires both individuals to be equally committed. It requires both individuals to give their all. Only when a man is 100% faithful to his woman does he begin to appreciate every feature, every expression and every flaw. It is at that point she then becomes the definition of true beauty. The pursuit of true love requires patience and a dependence on God. Many people like the idea of love but are not willing to put in the necessary work to accomplish real love.

Many people blame their indiscretions on some void in their relationship or some unmet need. But the fact of the matter is cheating is a choice often times made even when things are going right in a relationship. A lot of men won't fulfill their potential because they lack the discipline it takes to avoid temptation. But if you can settle down with one woman and give the rest of your energy to your goals, you will get everything you desire.

Nobody wins when you cheat. If you are not ready for love, don't break hearts in the process. Recognize areas where your flesh is weak and be mature enough to spare hearts instead of leaving a trail of shattered hearts. With the access we have to beautiful people, it is a must that we keep the full armor on. Even the best of us get tempted, however it is one thing to be tempted and it is a completely different ordeal to act. In all you do, flee from temptation.

Women settle far too often just to avoid being alone. Stop settling!! Being cheated on is not normal. Being lied to, is not normal. Being controlled and emotionally abused is not normal. The *Love & Hip Hop* generation has bred some bad habits and some flawed values and morals. Sharing your partner, your significant other sexually with someone else, is not normal. Crying and arguing more than you laugh and smile is not normal so stop suffering and settling for what is not normal.

Put a Ring On It

It takes absolutely no effort to engage in the following: playing house, shacking up making babies and imitating marriage. However, it does take a real man, a devoted man, a man of courage to meet you at the altar, stay committed to his vows, stay faithful to God and honor you as his wife for the rest of his life. Some people in the *Love & Hip Hop* generation, on some levels, despise marriage. They don't get married anymore, instead preferring to shack up and play house, have a baby and hope for the best. Then, of course, we begin to have relationship trials and tribulations, start doing the most and eventually speak down on the name of 'Love' and the office of marriage not acknowledging that it is our fault because we did it wrong from the jump, we did it wrong from the very beginning.

To those of you that feel like I am throwing shade, trust me, I'm not. A lot of what I described was once me. Shacking up and shunning marriage was the exact mode in which I operated which is why I qualify to speak on exactly why some men avoid getting married. I personally never saw a reason to get married. In fact, I was perfectly fine being a bachelor, enjoying my success and the many beautiful women it afforded me.

In no way was my path the right one. Although I do not have any kids of my own, which is only by the grace of God might I add, I didn't "wait" or "abstain" from sex before marriage. In fact, I jumped off the porch at a very young age and accumulated an extensive resume by the time I exchanged my vows. I shacked up also. I shacked up as a means to achieve some financial relief and not have to pay every single bill by myself. I also shacked up to stay connected to my future spouse. I know with a 100% certainty that if I had the liberty and the freedom that comes with having your own place, I would have pushed marriage well into my mid or late 30's. So by no means am I perfect and I know very well the struggle. However, when you know better, you do better!

When living like heathens we often turn away from God. The first thing we neglect is worship; we abandon the Lord. For me, I desired to strengthen my walk with Christ and along the journey I began to understand what the Word of God had to say about marriage and about cohabitation. Trying to be pleasing in His eyes and trying to do God's will while on this side, I began to examine my own ways! In doing so, I have gained infinite wisdom and revelation about how I should be conducting myself as a man. In Hebrews 13:4 for instance we are reminded, "Let marriage be held in honor among all, and let the marriage bed be undefiled, for God will judge the sexually immoral and adulterous." Or like was stated in 1 Corinthians 7:2 – "But because of the temptation to sexual immorality, each man should have his own wife and each woman her own husband." 1 Corinthians 6:18-20 – "Flee from sexual immorality. Every other sin a person commits is outside the body, but the sexually immoral person sins against his own body. Or do you not know that your body is a temple of the Holy Spirit within you, whom you have from God? You are not your own, for you were bought with a price. So glorify God in your body." These along with various other passages from the bible helped shape my view and my thinking as it related to marriage. The impact was profound. It allowed me to begin helping men and young couples 35 and under living in the *Love & Hip Hop Era* in this area of their life.

The PUT A RIGN ON IT Initiative

What is the "PUT A RING ON IT" Initiative?

In summary, The PUT A RING ON IT" initiative specifically targets men 35 and under who are single and contemplating marriage or men currently in a relationship delaying marriage. It is designed to: Encourage young couples to get married, have real conversations about the benefits of marriage, discuss the downside of shacking up, and overcome fear of commitment and much more.

For nearly five years now, the "PUT A RING ON IT" initiative has provided me a vehicle that has allowed me to pour into young men, specifically black men ages 35 and under that are either single and holding out on love or in a relationship but refuse to get married.

Although considered by many to be a relationship expert, I willingly admit, I was the least likely of all men to get married. I do, however, believe "If you are over 35, in a relationship for three or more years with a person and you are still not married, you know better!!! You are playing games and typically I don't seek to consult guys like that because as a man, you know better."

The "PUT A RING ON IT" initiative was birthed because I decided to be to other young men what I wished someone was to me. "Married men I knew, never kept it real when asked about what married life is like." The number one answer every man gave was "It's tough. Marriage is tough. It's hard work." As a young man who did not think marriage was for him, that answer only pushed me further away from even desiring to get married and left me with more questions: How is marriage tough? Why is marriage tough? What makes it tough? I wondered. – No man…Not one, ever answered this question. No man ever kept it real.

Now older and wiser, I believe I now know the reasons why men never offered much. Most of them weren't living right. They weren't doing right and most likely had a woman on the side. As a speaker who travels the country to speak about love and relationships, I often say God can't use you if He can't trust you. And talks about how to be young-married-and-faithful has afforded me many opportunities I otherwise would not have.

Today, when I meet with young men, my questions are simple and to the point. Always firm, most times I ask two questions (especially when I meet a young man that is currently in a relationship with a good woman): "What is the hold up?" and/or "What are you afraid of?" From there, men are usually able to open up and openly discuss their fears and/or their hesitations as well as, ask any questions of me they have about the benefits of getting married. For me, it is about having a dialogue. It is more about a conversation. Many times, young men just need someone to talk to; somebody that knows, and someone who is going to tell them the truth and keep it real.

As a former Division I athlete who holds a Master's degree and trained in Cognitive Behavioral Therapy, I tend to be honest. I share with others that I have a past with a variety of beautiful women. The experiences with women date back to high school and college (Michigan State University, Saginaw Valley State University and Wayne State University). Now married and a devoted husband, I remind people in all audiences, "I was who I was and I am who I am and I'm cool with both people." The old me no longer exists and because I speak from a place of lived experience, I challenge young men about, they quickly know, after about 2 minutes of talking to me, (whether they know my past or not) they know I understand this thing called love on a level that only a person who actually lived it can speak to on such a high level and in such a profound way."

Faithful

Salute to the men who still know how to be faithful and realize having that one woman who will stand by you through whatever, beats anything else.

A man will treat you how he sees you and how he sees you will be determined by how you treat yourself. Being faithful is nothing more than a matter of the mind. It becomes a battle of the mind when you allow lust and temptation to overtake you. When lust of the eye and temptation of the mind is working in harmony, the flesh gets weak. When the flesh gets weak one becomes more susceptible to the advances of the one pursuing you.

Only when a man is 100% faithful to his woman does he begin to appreciate every feature, every expression and every flaw. It is at that point she then becomes the definition of true beauty. Everything positive a man does for his woman also benefits him. If he shows her affection, she will show him more. If he protects her, she will soothe and comfort him more. Provide a woman with what she needs and she will work hard to give a man what he wants. Love and respect her and he will reap the benefits of her trust and loyalty.

I was a womanizer for many years. I didn't necessarily struggle with being faithful, however I ran away from commitment. In my mind, commitment meant being accountable and to me, being accountable often required a commitment. At the time, to be honest, being committed just felt like too much responsibility. As men, we are created to be with one person however the ills of the world, negative influences, peer pressure and being a slave to an image tells us we have to have a variety of women in order to be considered a real man. As young men who are often forced to abandon their childhoods and are unable to live and do the things that normal aged kids do, there was no honor in being faithful. Nobody ever praised a man for being faithful to one woman. However, as a young man living fast and looking to die young, it was almost like a rite of passage or a badge of honor to have, be seen or be known for having multiple women. Whether right or wrong, being a player was socially acceptable. Everyone from adults, to teachers to coaches, reinforced the behavior by celebrating you and anointing you. To be honest, growing up I did not see or know that anything was wrong with being a player.

Nowadays, of course, it is considered immoral and improper for someone married to have more than one sexual partner. Yet and still, many men and women, for that matter, have a hard time being faithful. I have discovered that being faithful is a mindset. People who decide to be faithful, you know, those of us living in today's world where everything is permissible even though it may not be beneficial have one commonality at the core of why they are faithful and that is, faithful people have determined that they love and respect their spouse too much to let feelings of lust cause them to cheat. Once I grew up, matured a little and decided to settle down and ultimately get married, I vowed to stay committed to my Queen. I made a promise to myself that I would not cheat on my wife and that I would remain faithful to my wife because I did not want to subject her to the public and/or private humiliation. That is why I am faithful.

I know many men, the ones I have seen fall from grace, have been the ones who were unfaithful to their wives. In the *Love & Hip Hop Era* we have very few positive male role models and even fewer married and faithful men worth emulating. I made up in my mind that if I was going to join the marriage club, I wanted to standout, do it my way, be different and be faithful to mine. Not only as a young married couple is our marriage strong, vibrant and alive, but God is at the center of our love. In real life and on social media, I hope I have modeled a standard for what young real love is and what a faithful marriage looks like; it is my wife's and I pleasure to inspire others through love.

Over the years, during my "PUT A RING ON IT" initiative, I have spoken to many men who had affairs on their spouse; some rarely, almost inadvertently, and also others who were repeat offenders. It is not easy to know why they have been unfaithful. One problem, however, is that they rarely know themselves and what motivates them. I have also noticed, on the other hand, that the men who are faithful seem to fall into the following different, somewhat overlapping, groups:

1. Some men simply have very little interest in sex, within or outside the marriage. I think that these are the men who have set down the various rules against different kinds of sexual behavior.

2. Some men are shy. They may be in a position where an opportunity appears for an illicit sexual encounter; and they, sort of, don't react until afterwards. Sometimes they report these minor encounters to me with a vague sense of regret (not really much regret, however.)

3. Most men who are faithful are simply too busy in their lives to have much time for an affair. They are preoccupied with work, dealing with kids and a home and/or being involved in various social activities. Having an affair seems too time-consuming and not worth the effort. Most of these men aren't thinking of affairs in the first place.

4. Some men say they feel uncomfortable lying and practicing the various complicated deceits required to successfully pull off having an affair.

5. Some men say that the stakes are too high. They know that their wives would feel terrible if they were caught being unfaithful; and, possibly, their marriages would be over or at least at risk.

Two takeaways: Whether men or women have affairs, in my experience, they seem to be no relationship to whether or not their sexual relationship with their spouse is good or bad. Some unfaithful men report, for instance, that sex with their wives is fine. Some men have had no sex with their wives for years. Some of them are very unhappy with their state of affairs, but as a group they seem unlikely to go through the trouble of having sex outside of marriage.

When the subject of having an extra-marital affair comes up, men who do not have affairs give some version of the reasons given above for not doing so. Surprisingly, considering what one hears in religious or political settings, very few men say that they are faithful because that is the only morally correct way to live, or they are faithful because that is what their religion tells them.

Don't Stay for the sake of the kids

Is your significant other abusing you? Emotional, verbal, or physically abusive relationships are just as traumatic for the children inside the home. Trust me, you are not doing your kids any favors by staying and allowing them to witness the abuse you are suffering.

Never let a man tell you twice that he does not want you. Never let a man put his hands on you in a violent or aggressive manner. You guys are supposed to be teammates, not enemies. If anything, you should be working together for the sake of the kids. You are in a relationship to smile, to laugh, to be happy and make memories. You shouldn't constantly be arguing, upset and crying. Sometimes having a kid together with a person you are no longer in love with or in a relationship with, complicates things and can cloud your judgment. As a rule of thumb, always do right by the children involved first. In addition, make sure your health and safety is also a top priority. Unfortunately, no matter how great of a woman you are, you will never be good enough to the man who is not ready.

When a woman is loved correctly, she becomes ten times the woman she was before. However, there is nothing cool nor honorable about being in an abusive relationship. In the *Love & Hip Hop* generation, everybody is looking for love. I get it. I know. But it takes a strong woman to remain single in a world that is accustomed to settling with anything just to say she has something. As I often say, it is better to be single and happy than to be in an abusive relationship settling for less. And it is certainly far better to be single than it is to be in a relationship where you are being lied to, cheated on and disrespected.

A man should never disrespect the mother of his child. No matter how mad you are, always remember she is doing whatever she can and the best she can to provide, protect, love and feed your child like no one else will, especially when you are inconsistent and barely lending a helping hand. And just because a person does not put hands on you, doesn't mean they are not abusive. Insults, disrespect and hurtful words are also forms of abuse. As a man, you can say sorry and promise it will never happen again all you want, but if your actions do not change, your words mean nothing.

Staying together for the sake of the kids won't do them any good when they grow up in a home watching two people in a toxic relationship that no longer know how to love each other. People think the most painful thing in life is losing the one you value, but the truth is, the most painful thing in life is losing yourself in the process of valuing someone too much and forgetting that you are special too.

Someone who truly loves you won't keep hurting you. Love makes you feel better not bitter. You deserve to be loved fully, regardless of your flaws. Somebody who loves you wouldn't put themselves in a position to lose you. Bottom line: Abuse is unacceptable!

Some people think that holding on makes you stronger, but sometimes letting go reveals your real strength. Ladies, when you love you, you won't tolerate someone else mistreating you, disrespecting you or isolating you. Because when you love you, the person you love has to meet your expectations. So, love yourself enough to stop giving certain people, second and third chances, when there are others still waiting in line for their first chance.

Sometimes the best reason to let go of a toxic relationship is because your child is watching. At the end of the day, you are a good woman, not perfect by any means, but your intentions are good, your heart is pure and you love hard with everything you have. And it is because of those qualities that you are worth it. Always have been; always will be.

Healing Takes Time

You've been a good woman to the wrong man. The worst thing you can do is listen to what she has been through then put her through it again.

At some point and time during a relationship, we all will experience hurt. There are several things that lead to hurt in a relationship. Lying and cheating, for instance, comes to mind as well as physical and verbal abuse. Remember, you are in a relationship to laugh, to be happy and to make memories. You should not be constantly arguing, upset and crying. Hurt people hurt people. And typically, broken people can't repair broken people, which is how the cycle of hurt continues.

God bless the woman who just wants to be better, do better, feel better and refuses to give up despite the hell she experiences on earth. Hurt happens when one is taken for granted. Having said that, never take the love of a good woman for granted. At some point she will quit; simply throw in the towel. Don't expect her to stick around forever dealing with disrespect, lack of appreciation, lack of attention and emotional abuse. A woman puts up with a lot... When she leaves, just remember, she didn't leave you for making too many mistakes. Typically, women, when they reach their breaking point, leave because you continued to make the same mistake too many times.

Part of why healing from past hurt takes time is because of the perpetual cycle one continues to exhibit. Cheaters will always accuse you of cheating. Liars will always accuse you of lying. Insecure people will make you feel insecure. Pay close attention to how people treat you. It is a reflection of who they really are. As I often say, when people treat you like they don't care, believe them, they don't.

Often times the deepest of a woman's insecurities comes from the men who have hurt them. It is important to remember that "love" and "hurt" are not related. See, love did not hurt you. Someone that did not know how to love hurt you. Don't confuse the two.

One day it just clicks...You realize what is important and what is not. You learn to care less about what other people think of you and more about what you think of yourself. You realize how far you have come and you remember when you thought things were such a mess that they would never recover. And then you smile. You smile because you are truly proud of yourself and the person you have fought hard to become. No person has the right to condemn you for how you repair your heart or how long you choose to grieve, because no one knows how much you are hurting. Recovering takes time and everyone heals at their own pace.

No matter how busy a person's day may be, if they really care, they'll always find time for you. Lack of quality time spent was part of what led to the divorce of my mom and dad after 23 years of marriage. Add some infidelity and some verbal abuse combined with her low self-esteem and you have a recipe for disaster. I watched my mom go through the toughest time of her life, I watched her experience both public and private humiliation, most of which was brought on by her thinking and what she believed others were saying about her and the divorce. But nevertheless, her feelings were her feelings. She has never really truly moved on although she is in a much better place mentally and spiritually. It took her between six to eight years to fully heal. In that moment I learned, if it wasn't for the struggle you wouldn't have the strength. God is always building you even when it seems like He is breaking you. Never let someone put a timetable on how long it takes you to heal from the hurt you've experienced.

You are a good hearted woman. You have been hurt over and over again. And you would expect you to be heartless by now but your heart is so full of love that you continue to love deeply. All you need is a good person that will cherish you and give your heart the love that it deserves.

Part 5

Loving the wrong person

We sometimes love the wrong person, cry over the wrong person, but one thing is for certain, getting it wrong, helps us find the right person. Seek someone that is not only proud to have you, but will cherish every opportunity to be with you. Never settle. Wait and know that anything worth having is worth waiting for. It takes a strong person to remain single in a world that is accustomed to settling for anything just to say they have something. When you meet that person that sticks by you despite how difficult you are, keep them. Hold on to them at all cost because finding that one who cares enough to look past your flaws does not happen every day. In the end our biggest regret is not that we were hurt. It is living with the fact we allowed pain to change us. There is still time to bounce back. Don't stay where heartbreak left you.

Many women mistakenly believe that they have to change what is on the outside in order to be beautiful. But changing your outside appearance will not matter if you still feel inadequate on the inside. Ladies, the truth is that you do not have to change the way you look, you simply have to change your outlook. You have to change the way you view and talk to yourself. High self-esteem is the most attractive quality you can have.

No one can see how incredible you are if you cannot see it yourself. When it comes to love, it is never too late to realize what is important in your life and fight for it.

Ladies, surrender your heart to the Lord. Stop letting men fill voids, brokenness and loneliness. Wait for someone who will love you consistently. Evict those from your life who say one thing and do another. Inconsistent people break hearts. You may never understand how the person you let your guard down for and gave your heart to, ends up being the same person who broke your heart. Sometimes you meet someone, and it is so clear that the two of you, on some level, belong together as lovers, as friends, or as family or something entirely different. It just clicks. You sometimes meet people throughout your life who out of nowhere, under the strangest circumstances help you to feel alive. I don't know if that makes me believe in coincidence, fate, or sheer blind luck, but it definitely makes me believe in something.

There may be times you may feel like you wasted years in a relationship that did not work out. But God can place someone into your life so great, so fun, so friendly, and so attractive, that you do not even remember the years you lost.

Still wondering if you are loving the wrong person? If your man is unemployed, refuse to look for work and plays the video game all day, unplug the game and tell him to get out! And if you have a child or children, you do not need them emulating laziness. Ladies, you cannot change a man that does not see anything wrong with his actions. A real man would never risk losing his relationship with you because he wants to play video games. A real man would never hide his relationship with you. Every woman deserves to have a man who is proudly willing to say to the world, "yup, she is my one and only. She is beautiful and she is mine." No one ever gets tired of loving. They just get tired of waiting, assuming, hearing lies, saying sorry and hurting.

Pray for your future spouse

It is important to pray about the person you are interested in. God just might reveal something that will save you from heartbreak. God will send someone who knows how to love and care for your heart the way you have always desired. If a man is not following God, he is not fit to lead. If he does not have a relationship with God, he will not know how to have a relationship with you. In the *Love & Hip Hop* generation, a consistent worship life is the number one thing missing in relationships. We now live in a society where we want what we see on television. We desire to have the types of relationships we see on reality television not knowing they are the furthest thing from resembling real love and that the majority of them are broken and lost. Live your life. Find your mate, that special someone that was designed specifically for you and pray for that person.

Pray for your future spouse. God is working on their heart just like He's working on yours. Trust God and His perfect timing. God will never give you the wrong person, so when someone is not staying with you, acknowledge that it may be God trying to save you. Rejection is for your protection. Too often times, we try to hold on to something that we should have let go of a long time ago. This can lead to unnecessary heartache. Love is not hard. There is nothing difficult about love.

So, if trying to love someone feels like it is hard, then it is not love.

Be ready and willing to accept the flaws and the baggage a person brings to the relationship. Your job is not to change them, your job is to love them and that means loving them for who they are, flaws and all. Many times we go through tough times that lead to quitting on relationships and marriages all because we desire a perfect person. I am here to tell you, we are all imperfect people and the perfect person does not exist. That is why it is imperative you sit at the feet of the Lord and pray about the one you desire to be with.

When someone is not treating you right, no matter how much you love them, you have to love yourself more and walk away. He is going to be sorry he lost you, so stop worrying. Most relationships end because one person is often times giving more and doing more than the other. Love requires both people to give 100%. There are no short cuts in love. If someone is taking you and your love for granted, it may be time for you to move on. But remember, take all of your burdens to God. Let Him reveal to you whether or not you need to move on, or if you need to stay and try to make it work. You should be praying for your spouse every day and every night. That is how deep it is. That is how serious this thing is.

Many men, even when they are not doing right are vocal about the woman they love. Therefore, a man who does not make it clear that he loves you and wants to be with you, is also a man who doesn't deserve you. On the other end of the spectrum, however, never miss out on a good person that can make your life great just because they are a little difficult. The good ones never come easy. As a man, I know you are tired. I know you are physically and emotionally drained but you have to keep going. While hurting and dealing with your own pain, never push away the one who truly loves you to the point of no return. Many women, although they may love hard are just as capable of letting go even harder. Some relationships are meant to be seasonal. Know that. Understand that. And be okay with that. Don't break your own heart trying to make another person permanent. One of the hardest decisions you will ever face in life is choosing to try harder or walk away. If you prayed about it, then there is no need to worry about it.

When someone is not treating you right, no matter how much you love them, you have to love yourself more and let go. Typically men don't act right or change until they are either embarrassed by their actions or they see you have moved on and found someone new. Only then do they cherish you and attempt to do all the things they refused to do when they had you. Unfortunately, by then, sometimes it is too late. He is going to be sorry he lost you to another man and will wish he had done the things he was now allowing another man to do for you. When the right person comes along, you will know. Everything about the person will feel right. Everything about your relationship will be right, things will just flow, naturally and organically. Enjoy it. Relish in it and know that is all because of God. Forget the past, let go of the pain and remember what an incredible woman you are.

Be with someone who thanks God for you. A good man will recognize how precious you are when you recognize it for yourself. Regardless of what type of relationship you are in and regardless of the pain and suffering you have endured, never stop praying. Your prayer may prevent a breakdown and foster a breakthrough. Your prayer may deliver a person from their addiction or lead them to the help they need. You may be the only person that is or that has prayed for your spouse or your significant other. It might be your prayer that causes him to return to the Father and rediscover his purpose. Pray and do not cease.

Modern Romance (Online Dating)

A few months ago, while gathering my thoughts for my book, I was sitting at a coffee shop reading and responding to emails when the woman next to me did something a little odd. Surrounded by unknown people, she pulled out her phone, and very covertly, in a real low-key manner, hid her iPhone beneath the counter, and with me being just a little bit nosey because of how awkward she was acting, I could see that she opened up an online dating app. On her screen, pictures of men appeared and then disappeared to the left and right, depending on the direction in which she swiped.

What in the world?! I couldn't help but wonder to myself, is this what online dating is? Is this what it has done to us? Is it creating a new reality in which people actively avoid real-life interactions?

Of course, I am not alone in my initial thinking, as others have expressed worry about these sorts of questions before as well. The fear that online dating is changing us, that it's creating diminished social skills, unhealthy habits and preferences that aren't in our best interests, is being driven more by paranoia than it is by actual facts.

There are a lot of theories out there about how online dating is bad for us and mostly every theory has been unfounded.

One of the first things you have to know and understand in the *Love & Hip Hop Era* is how dating (which is now commonly referred to as courting since not everyone calls it dating) has impacted changed over time. Today, the age of marriage in the United States has increased dramatically over the years. You see, people used to get married in their early 20s, which meant that most dating that was done, or most courting that was done, was done with the intention of settling down right away. Well, that is not the life or the mindset that young people born in the *Love & Hip Hop Era* lead anymore. The average age of first marriage is now in the late twenties, and more people in their 30s and even 40s are deciding not to settle down. Many people have embraced single-living.

However, with the rise of phone apps, social media and online dating websites, people have access to more potential partners than they could meet at work or at church. It makes it easier for someone who is looking for something very specific in a partner to find what they are looking for. It also helps the people who use the apps by allowing them to enjoy a pattern of regular hookups that do not have to lead to a relationship. I think these things are definitely characteristic of modern romance in the *Love & Hip Hop Era.*

The concerns about online dating comes from theories about how too much choice might be bad for you. The idea is that if you are faced with too many options you will find it harder to pick one, that too much choice is overwhelming. We see this in catch-all-restaurants — if there are too many things to choose from on the menu while trying to decide what you want to eat, for instance, you might feel that it's just too complicated to consider to pick one option, therefore, you might end up deciding that it is not worth settling for just one thing.

I am not sure if that theory, even if it is true, applies to dating, especially not in the *Love & Hip Hop Era*. To be honest, I actually do not see any negative consequences for people who meet partners online. In fact, studies show that people who meet their partners online are not more likely to break up. Once you are in a relationship with somebody, it does not matter how you met that other person. Nobody cares. There is no real evidence that shows people who meet online are worse off. In fact, although online dating is not my preference, some studies have shown that online dating has real benefits. For the single person who has a hard time finding partners in their real every-day life, the larger pool of potential partners online is a huge advantage for them. For individuals who are meeting people every day, especially younger people in their early twenties, online dating is alive and well and it has really become a viable option for people in thin dating markets that are not surrounded by much potential.

Basic human needs consist of the need for love, romance, relationships and sex and thanks to technology and the emergence of online dating, the ability to match people who would not have otherwise found each other has helped change a lot of people's relationship status on Facebook.

On average, approximately 70 percent of the people who meet online had no prior connection. None at all. They did not have friends in common and their families did not know each other. We are talking about perfect strangers here. Many people are thankful for online dating apps mainly because prior to the internet, it was nearly impossible for complete strangers to meet. It just did not happen. It was very unlikely before all of this technology. Although I am happily married and no longer in search of my soulmate, the one real benefit of social media, apps and internet searches is being able to find people you might have things in common with but otherwise would never have crossed paths with.

6 Facts about Online Dating people don't want to talk about

These facts come from a friend of mine and are based on her experiences with online dating. I asked her to provide an alternative outlook so that I could cover both ends of the spectrum related to online dating, the good and the bad. In no way am I suggesting that it is impossible to find love online. Some of the weirdest people have won the mega-millions. I just happen to believe that online dating has been gassed up and although a viable option to finding a partner is not the ideal way to find long lasting, real love.

Fact #1: We go together? I Thought You Meant Sex!

Unclear messages and expectations is by far the biggest knock of online dating. Especially when you interacting with the opposite sex within a 50-miles or in the city you live in.

Regardless of what app you use, it makes no difference what category you set your profile to, men in particular, will still assume you want to have sex. It's unbelievable at times.

She recalled meeting a guy she chatted online with for several weeks prior and he told her half-way through their dinner date that he was looking forward to spending the night at her place. Come again? She said. He kindly informed her that he was staying at her place. Call it wishful thinking or whatever you want but needless to say, he did not get his way.

It appeared that a lot of men out there assume the "date" is just part of the process of going through the motions to get to the bedroom where they are hoping it goes down at. This can happen on any date, regardless if you met online or not. However, this happened to her so frequently that she began to question whether meeting a guy online sent a subliminal message that sex was on the menu even though it was never discussed and her profile indicated she was interested in serious relationships only.

It is safe to assume that the actual number of people using online dating apps are really looking to score rather than find true love.

Fact #2: Stretching the Truth.

It is no secret, people can be whoever they want to be online and furthermore, people can say whatever they want about themselves online. I have seen it all on social media. Some job description says Point Guard for the NBA, others are CEO's of organizations that do not exist or that are not registered within the state they reside. Studies have already indicated that both men and women stretch the truth about different things on their profile. Women tend to lie about their weight and men tend to lie about their height and salary.

Some men have shared with me time and time again that when they finally met a woman they had been talking to online, she turned out to be at least 30 lbs. heavier than she stated on her profile. Reminds me of the movie Friday, when Smokey, who was played by actor Chris Tucker met a woman who said she looked like the R&B sensation Janet Jackson but was big, Smokey said she looked more like Freddie Jackson. I still laugh out loud every time I watch that movie and especially that part! Sadly, it is not the actual weight that bothers a man so much as the lying about it!

Catfishing is at an all-time high. Some people, both men and women don't even use their own pictures! In the *Love & Hip Hop Era*, "Fake is the new Real." Nothing builds love and trust like lying about who you are and putting up a picture of someone else declaring to be that person, if you put a picture up at all.

People stretch the truth about whether they are single, if they have kids, their job, their income, the city they live in, you name it. But how are you supposed to know if they are keeping it real or not? It is a lot different when you know them from the gym or from work and if you are friends on social media, because you could always do some investigative work about whether they are in fact single, or has a boo, what they do for a living and where they live. Online however, especially with no profile picture and false information, that is very hard to do. You have no choice but take their word and hope they are who they claim to be.

Fact #3: It is Your Turn to Visit Me: Long Distance Dating

A friend of mine said that she met a guy online and tried the whole long-distance thing with him. She was a Diva! Too needy. Required too much attention for a long-distance relationship. Needless to say, it did not work out. The truth of the matter is, long-distance relationships are not for everybody.

Certain situations and certain types of relationships require a different kind of sacrifice but there is a huge difference between meeting someone, dating that person for at least three or four months and then due to unforeseen circumstances i.e. job relocation, etc., you two are forced to do the long distance thing versus trying to get to know someone online that lives on the other side of the country.

One of the best ways to get to know someone is not by listening to everything they have to say about themselves but by seeing how they interact with you in real life, face-to-face and with other people and in different settings. This is really hard to accomplish online and especially if that online relationship is long distance. Unfortunately there will be no dinner dates or long walks on the beach anytime soon.

In long-distance relationships with people you met online but have never me in real life, there is no way of knowing if anything that person has said about themselves or in their profile is accurate, i.e., "photographer" and you also don't know if that person is in a relationship with someone else or several other people.

Fact #4: It was over at First Sight

Nothing is more crushing to a person's self-esteem than building up the courage to meet someone they like only to have that person take one look at them and "chuck up the deuces, and say hey, I have to go pick up my momma from work. I'll catch up with you later."

Posting real pictures of yourself on your profile is not even a guarantee. People can look different in real life compared to how they look online. The issue with online dating is that when you do finally decide to meet, there can be so much emphasis on appearance and how a person looks that one is unable to get passed aesthetics in order to get to know the person. Many people, unfortunately believe that if sparks are not flying at hello, that there can be no hope of any romance in the future. That is very unfortunate.

One reason "meet-ups" often fall apart is because as people we tend to have a certain standard and when those standards are not met, we feel let down. We have all been there. It is so easy to create this fantasy of someone in our mind, especially when we are basing everything off of that perfect picture in their online profile and what they have told us about themselves. You bring your own standards to the table, hoping this potential Adam or Eve will meet your list of requirements, but in reality, living up to your standards is impossible to do.

Fact #5: Online, Who You Are Is Not Enough

Being you is not enough and is one of the main reasons why online dating can be dangerous to your mental and emotional health and self-esteem.

Of course when we go out on a date we do not show up in pajamas and a head scarf on. Typically we try to make a good first impression by putting on a new outfit, or get a fresh haircut. But there is a huge difference between looking good and trying to be somebody you are not. At times, the online dating scene sends the message to people that who you are is not good enough.

The Dr. Phils of online dating try to provide directions on what to say and what not to say about yourselves in our profiles. For example, "If you say _____ you will come across as thirsty!" Instead they instruct you to be more like, "The woman that loves Sunday football, is every man's dream girl. Be that woman online." Why not be the woman that will attract the guy you want? Time and time again you are sent the message that you need to improve yourself or else your Adam or your Eve will never look your way.

Fact #6: Looks Shall Always Triumph Over Personality

Just like in the work place, online dating has a tendency to favor people who look good and are deemed more attractive even if they have no substance and very little to offer in the way of personality or character. Unfortunately, having a great personality means nothing compared to a big booty and pretty eyes.

Online dating seems to be more about meeting someone to hang out and have fun with, not finding someone to have a serious relationship with. For some men and women, it is very frustrating when you are unable to find someone you are compatible with.

In the *Love & Hip Hop Era* a tremendous amount of importance is placed on how someone looks instead of who a person is. It is difficult to truly get to know a person's character over the internet. For instance, opening doors or being respectful towards women is demonstrated better in person than online.

For women who are not Instagram models, it can be flat out discouraging to post the real you online only to have zero or maybe one response. Unfortunately, a twerk video or a *thirst trap* picture of yourself in a position showing cleavage, or in your panties and bra will definitely get more reactions from men. Yes, men are visual, but women who are serious about finding their Adam or having a serious relationship want a guy to be interested in more than her bra size.

Final Thoughts on Online Dating

By now I have probably turned you off from finding love online but it means more to me that you know what you are up against when it comes down to online dating. Being single is hard enough without the added element of the unknown when dealing with complete strangers who might reject you as well.

It is not impossible to find love and serious relationships online but your chances are very bleak regardless if you are a male or female, so do not reject the traditional way of getting to know someone at the gym, at church or at work.

Why Strong women leave good men

Women tend to invest a lot in a relationship; they put their hearts and soul into it. They trust blindly, care immensely and love recklessly. Most women don't put themselves first when they are truly in love. My home girl fell in love with a guy who treated her wrong in so many ways. She trusted him and gave him everything she had. She refused to look past the false image she had created of him for herself. Her idea of a perfect relationship was petty and shallow. She didn't realize the wrong she was doing to herself; until she was finally out of the relationship.

Men, if and when chosen, want to be selected by a strong independent woman; the kind of woman who knows her worth, that respects herself and knows how to make others respect her. The moment a woman learns to love and respect herself, she gains the ability to evaluate her relationship better and make better choices. She prepares herself to leave the man she loves, not because she is not loyal but because she what she is and is not willing to put up with. Every meaningless thing suddenly starts to make sense. Below are some of the reasons that make women leave the men they love.

1. Lack of common interests are not a good sign

Okay, before I say anything, I want you to know that people change with time. The person you are with changes every day!! You change every day! It might be you or it might be your partner. Having said that, although it is very true that opposites attract you both should have some common qualities and interests. It is *common interests* that initially helped you both bond whose absence will have a drastic effect on your relationship. My home girl's ex used to adore so many things about her but, by the end of the relationship, her guy started to disapprove of almost everything she did. Any girl would be left questioning her decisions.

2. Lack of communication will kill you

Women need someone to talk to, it is nearly impossible for a guy to be by her side all the time but if you are not present and gone most of the time, you are giving her one less reason to hold on. If you are not with her every time she needs you, it's almost like asking her to leave. My home girl's ex-guy would go missing for days without any explanation.

Please note: "being there" means that you need to be mentally and emotionally present. You need to "listen" to her, not just nod your head at everything she says while playing the X-box. Pay attention, become a valid part of the conversation and make the conversation lively. That's the only way you can strengthen communication between the two of you and make your relationship stronger.

3. Physical Intimacy is very important

Women need just as much physical intimacy as men. If you stop making sexual advances or are not taking care of her needs, she is probably going to think that there is someone else who is taking care of your desires for you. She is probably going to feel unwanted and worthless which will be very damaging for your relationship.

Being physically intimate says a lot of things to your woman. Yes, not everyone who gets-it-in is in love, but love is the number one reason people have sex. If you care about your partner and their needs in bed, women will have an assurance that your relationship is something worth holding on to and that there is something still there between you two.

Please Note: Don't confuse LOVE with LUST. I'm not talking about lust here. Lust can only survive for a while, love stays forever. You can only feel lust for someone for so long, and then it will go away and you won't be attracted to them anymore. When you love someone, you are holistically attracted to them, and it's natural.

4. Selfishness takes over

You are more invested into activities that please you, the less time you give her, the more distant she starts to feel which hurts your relationship. Women want to be and like to be a priority, not an option. They don't want to be treated as a part-time chick or a side chick. If you want to do you and be left alone, she will eventually pick up on the vibes and energy you're giving off and after that she will seriously consider leaving you alone for good.

Remember, a relationship is an amalgam of things connected to one another giving you both reasons to hold on to one another. If these connections don't exist anymore, your lady will no longer feel inclined to stay by your side. The biggest thing a woman needs is assurance and security. If you aren't for filling your promises and putting effort into your relationship, it will pull her apart bit by bit, to a point that she wouldn't want to commit anymore and will probably look around for a new romance. A woman, unlike girls, doesn't believe in fairy tales. She is a practical person and even though she would be very much in love with you, she would run out of reasons to hold on and when she does she will walk away.

5. Insecurities

Insecurities slowly kill any and all relationships eventually. When a woman is insecure, everything and everybody, especially other females become a perceived threat. When a woman feels like her man is insecure, it's a huge turn off. A man should have faith and trust in his woman, he shouldn't be snooping around and he shouldn't be asking her a million questions every day. If THIS sounds like you or the person you are with it could be you are insecure about the person you claim you love. Insecure people ruin more relationships than texting and sexting...which is a totally different topic. Love comes with trust and trust kills insecurities. Learn to trust your partner!

6. Too many lies

Keep it 100. Matter-a-fact, keep it 1,000. If you follow me on social media, you know firsthand I'm going to keep it all the way real with you. It's not acceptable to lie to the person you love. Relationships are built on the trust and lying is just a way to throw your relationship out the window. Keeping up with lies at some point becomes hard work. One way or the other, your girl will eventually find out that you lied and that'll be the end of your relationship (or at least the trust they had for you will never be the same).

When you lie to someone once, not only is it a sign of disrespect but it also says a lot about how you really feel about your woman and your relationship. But more importantly, it means that you'll at some point lie to them again. If you don't want to drive your woman away from you, don't hide things, look sneaky, act guilty and don't lie. Speaking the truth may hurt them but speak truthfully and be honest!

Why Strong Women leave good men – Part 2

7. No personal space

One of my close female friends recently broke up with her guy because he smothered her and refuse to give her space. Couldn't go to the store, couldn't go get her nails done, couldn't do anything!!! Personal space is extremely vital for all of us. We can't be our true selves with others unless we get to spend personal and alone time with ourselves and do our own activities away from our significant other. "Doin You" and hanging out with your friends or people you are close to is necessary. If you want your woman to love and respect you more, give her the space she needs to grow on her own. It doesn't make you a bad boyfriend or husband if you let your girl have her space and do her own thing!

8. Being "unattached" or "emotionally unavailable"

Being unattached and emotionally unavailable is one of the worst things you can be to your significant other. She doesn't want you to just hang out with her, go to fancy dinners with her, watch a movie with her and be "absent" during all of these things. Your woman wants you to be emotionally involved, she wants you to understand. She wants your love and affection, not just your money and material assets.

People who are unattached and emotionally unavailable for too long from their significant other often end up being completely distant and disconnected. That's why I encourage you to be there for your woman, understand her struggles; encourage her, be her biggest fan. That's all she really wants.

9. Trying to change her

Remember, to love your woman for the person she is, not the person you want her to be. Everyone should be loved for who they are. You shouldn't be with someone who constantly wants to change everything about you. If the one you are with is trying to change you and refuse to love your imperfections, you will slowly become someone you are not and won't be able to recognize who you really are as a person.

Trying to change your woman, is an indication that you're not in love with her, but in love with the idea of her being the way you want her to be. People don't fall in love and intentionally try to change the people they love. Love is patient, love is kind. Love makes no excuses. When you truly and genuinely love someone, you love them for who they are and not what you can make them into. That sort of selfish love only leads to fights, arguments, regrets and unfortunately sometimes, breakups.

10. Not giving her enough quality time

Time is considered the most important commodity in the world. Time is one of the most precious gift you can give to the one you love. When you spend time with someone, you tell them that they're important to you and their presence means a lot to you. People who tend to be "always busy" often end up alone and in-and-out of relationships.

Avoid being the man who does not have enough time to spend with his significant other. If you're out here grinding and handling business, she will understand. But if you constantly develop a habit of not spending quality time with your woman and labelling it as "I'm just crazy busy right now", she is going to see right through you and the thought that "my man doesn't have any time for me" is going to hurt your woman more than anything.

11. Comparing her with others

Comparing your woman to another woman is the most common reason women leave the men they love. It is important to keep in mind that you can't compare one person to another. Everyone is unique and different in their own way and it is highly unfair to your woman if you're comparing them to your ex or someone else. Just as bad as comparing your partner is complaining. Complaining about what they don't do and how they are not like someone else is a recipe for disaster and a major turn off. It is also a quick way to make your woman feel like she's not appreciated for who she is. No one wants to feel like their every move will be judged or that they have to compete with others.

12. Ignoring the small things

It is the small things that matter. The fanfare is cool but not the most important thing to your woman. People who appreciate and pay attention to the small things are the people who will be happier in life. Those who appreciate the small things also find happiness in the little things. Those who only pay attention when it's something big, are the people who won't find long-term happiness. Learn to appreciate the small things and make your women feel appreciated.

ACKNOWLEDGMENTS

For me, the most difficult part of the writing process is writing the acknowledgments. There are so many people who inspire me and played a part in making this book a reality. I have been blessed with so many awesome people who have made such a profound impact on my life that trying to name them all is a bit overwhelming. I am extremely fortunate to have so many great friends and please know I mean that from the bottom of my heart. I thank God for you all daily because each of you have in many ways enriched my life. Thanks for the thoughtfulness, kind words, prayers and well wishes. I deeply appreciate you because you have often been the catalyst for needed change in my life and the impetus for introspection, and without you I don't know where I would be.

I'd be remiss if I did not mention the following individuals: My spiritual and life coach, Reverend Jerry Bishop. You have served as my spiritual mentor since I dedicated my life to Lord and made the choice to go hard for the Kingdom. You are like another father figure in my life and I appreciate your firm yet consistent love for me and other men navigating this thing called life. I am thankful for the friendship we have. It is a friendship filled not only with laughter but deep and transparent dialogue. A lot of times it has been therapeutic for me on what often feels like a solitary journey I am on. Although many would not understand will not understand the rich relationship we enjoy, I am reminded that what we have is not for everybody to understand. Sometimes God just places to people together that get it and understand each other. Thank you for your anointing, making me see the good in others, forcing me to think and provoking me to prayer.

A special thanks to my brothers, Preston and Jay. I know that collectively the three of us makes our mother proud on a daily basis. I am grateful for our friendship but our love for each other as brothers, business partners and sounding boards. Be able to call and/or text you has been a tremendous advantage for me. I could not have asked for better brothers than you.

To my son Anthony, who I love as if you were my biological son. I have enjoyed serving as your father and providing for you the necessary tools to be successful in life. My only hope is that I am around long enough to be there for you and with you during those difficult times life will bring. As a young man myself, I realize that being a man by far the toughest thing you will ever do. Understand, there were many before you and there will be many after you and none of us became a man without error. My hope is to lessen your learning curve by lessons I have shared in this book and also leading by example in our daily lives.

To my wife Corinthia: We have a special kind of love and it was so from the moment we met. We have endured a few tough times together and I during those moments I have come to realize that your soft and kind demeanor hides a very strong core at the center of who you are. You are my rock and have often been my strength. For that I thank you. I deeply admire how you handle adversity and the way you love our son. You have endured a lot beginning at a young age and to this day I am amazed at how you survived as well as how strong you are. Sometimes I think you are Superwoman. You effortlessly do the unthinkable time and time again. Undoubtedly, you are an extremely incredible woman and I am glad to tell the world you are all mine.

To my mother and my father, Glorie and Chris Sr.: I thank God for you every day because without each of you, there would be no me. I thank you for your unconditional love and support. Your unwavering spirit and love for others motivates me and has inspired me to live a life dedicated to inspiring others. I am joyed to know you were able to see the fruits of your labor and to witness some of the things I have accomplished so far. The best way for me to thank you both is by what I do with my life. It is my hope that you are proud. I could not have asked for better parents. I love you both dearly.

Thank you to Sean Gardner, my graphic designer for this entire project. You always treat me and my work with great dignity and integrity. To Shanda Vaughn, who served as my proof reader and editor, I thank you from the bottom of my heart. You would not allow me to put out a project that did not best represent the man you have come to know. I thank you for our friendship and I thank you for your continued support not only to myself but to my friends as well as my family. We appreciate you more than you know.

ABOUT CHRIS

Chris Sain Jr. a former Division I athlete turned educator and author. Considered by many to be one of the most influential people on social media, he is unapologetically real about love & relationships. A renowned speaker and community leader, many view Chris as a relationship expert however he explains that he only shares lived experiences with his audiences and with his readers in a way that many can relate to.

He never liked school but loved the ladies and excelled in sports. A Michigan State University student-athlete, Chris graduated at the top of his class with a BSW from Saginaw Valley State University and a MSW from Wayne State University. He wanted to demonstrate what he could accomplish when he put his mind to something.

Chris is a successful entrepreneur. He was named Top 40 under 40 Business Leaders by Grand Rapids Business Journal in 2014 and 2016. In addition to earning numerous accolades, Chris has gained wide recognition for maintaining a strong commitment to his faith and values. Remaining to his call has made Chris into an *Influencer* that redefines mainstream success.

He is the Co-Founder and CEO of Grand C.I.T.Y. Sports, Inc. a faith based, community driven, non-profit organization that targets at-risk youth by emphasizing education through sports. Chris is currently contemplating completing his PhD.

Chris resides in Grand Rapids, Michigan, with his wife Corinthia, and son Anthony.

CONNECT WITH ME ON SOCIAL MEDIA:

FACEBOOK: Chris Sain Jr.

INSTAGRAM: @Chris_Sain

TWITTER: @Chris_Sain

BLOG: chrissain.blogspot.com/

References:

Cai, H., Brown, J.D., Deng, C., & Oakes, M.A. (2007). Self-esteem and culture: Differences in cognitive self-evaluations or affective self-regard? Asian Journal of Social Psychology, 10, 162-170.

Campbell, W.K., Foster, C.A., & Finkel, E.J. (2002). Does self-love lead to love for others? A story of narcissistic game playing. Journal of Personality and Social Psychology, 83(2), 340-354.

Freire, E. (2013). The healing power of self-love. Therapy Today, 24(9), 34-35.

Holmes, L. (2014). Five science-backed reasons it's important to love yourself. The Huffington Post. Retrieved from http://www.huffingtonpost.com/2014/09/30/love-yourself-science-study_n_5900878.html

Neff, K. (2015). The five myths of self-compassion: What keeps us from being kinder to ourselves? Psychotherapy Networker Magazine, 39(5), 30-47.

Neff, K.D., & Beretvas, S.N. (2013). The role of self-compassion in romantic relationships. Self and Identity, 12, 78-98.

Made in the USA
Columbia, SC
15 December 2021

489021R00083